REACHING THE HEART OF GOD

The Key To Revival

by Mac Owen

with J. Arthur Lagoe

Aletheia Publishing

Aletheia Publishing
4712 Kingsway
Anacortes, WA 98221

Library of Congress Catalog Card Number: 96-085872

ISBN 0-9641761-1-4

Printed in the United States of America

DEDICATION

I would like to dedicate this book to my dearest friend, my loving wife and helpmate, Lollie. She has been at my side for over forty years, through thick and thin, when criticism and discouragement seemed overwhelming. She has truly been a gift from God, for which I am deeply grateful.

I would also like to dedicate this book to each minister and teacher that has sown God's Word into my life over the years. I fully acknowledge that much of the teaching in this book is from others who have planted God's Word into my heart.

Most important of all, I dedicate this book to the precious Holy Spirit of God, who makes all things possible through Christ Jesus our Lord.

REACHING THE HEART OF GOD
The Key to Revival

TABLE OF CONTENTS

FORWARD

Intense and strong determination are words that aptly describe the author, Mac Owen. We have worked together for many years, sometimes serving together on the mission field. From my observation, Mac and Lollie Owen are an epitome of true missionaries. Nothing is so difficult or uncomfortable that it restrains them from obeying God's command to go into all the world. The Word of God flows freely from Mac's heart and lips as he teaches and trains people in other lands. Whether in the jungles of headhunter country of the Philippines, or in the mud huts of Haiti, the lost sinner is held in rapt attention to the translator, as Mac so carefully explains the words of Jesus.

This book contains the feelings and devotions of a man and his wife who have consistently attempted to reach and please the heart of God. Soul winning has been the essence of their frequent travels to the various nations of the world, where they have compassionately ministered to the lost and hurting. The combined years of faithful service of both Mac and Lollie surely qualifies them to write on this subject, helping others understand the heart of God. They have "walked out" these principles in their own lives, and offer many first-hand illustrations from their experiences.

You will find a very special anointing from the words in this book. Read them with the expectation that God will give you a further dimension of understanding and thus bring a greater burden for evangelism and witnessing into your own life. Allow this book to be a training manual to assist you in your ministry calling. You will receive helpful insight and anointed revelations from the Holy Spirit, to help you become more effective and more committed in your walk with the Lord.

The reading of this book is a must for those already serving the Lord and to leaders preparing for service. You will be truly challenged and equipped for the front lines of ministry at home and abroad. Above all, you will learn how to reach the heart of God . . . and discover the key to revival.

Dr. Gerald Derstine, Chairman
Gospel Crusade, Inc. - Christian Retreat
Bradenton, Florida

GOD'S HAPPY HEART

Nestled down in the heart of God,
Is a work that's dear to Him.
It's done by those who win the lost,
And preserve their lights lest they grow dim.

God's heart is glad when the lost are saved,
And ransomed from their sins.
He rewards the ones who serve Him thus,
And gives them peace within.

But greater still remains the reward,
For those who make God glad.
This world is but a stepping stone,
To riches we've not had.

So take new faith for each today,
Stand strong in all you are.
For in that day when Christ returns,
You'll shine above the brightest star!

With heart-felt love the Father waits,
Till we the lost have won.
And when God's toll has reached the mark,
The celebration will have begun!

So see the heart of God rejoice,
And feel the joy He feels.
Thus be renewed with vision clear,
And let God's light your future seal.

Lydia Chorpening
used by permission

CHAPTER 1

THE HEART OF GOD

...the LORD has sought out a man after his own heart and appointed him leader of his people...

1 Samuel 13:14b

What is God's heart toward His people? In the above verse, God has rejected Saul as King of Israel and has chosen David to replace him. Why? Because, He says, David is *"a man after His own heart."* But how can we reach God's heart? The Bible says that God is spirit. Can a spirit even have a heart? Yes He can. The sixth chapter of Genesis speaks plainly of God's heart.

> *Then the Lord saw that the wickedness of man was great on the earth, and that every intent of the thoughts of his heart was only evil continually. And the Lord was sorry that He had made man on the earth, and He was grieved in His heart.* Genesis 6:5-6 NAS (emphasis added)

God created us to be different from all the rest of His creation. He created us in His own image, with thinking and reasoning minds and the ability to make choices. All other creatures are ruled by instinct, a preprogrammed pattern of responses that God built into them. Even the trees and the plants of the field grow and have their own cycles and seasons. But He gave man the free will to choose, to make his own decisions, to choose to do right or to do wrong. God took a great chance in doing so. Being omniscient (all knowing), He knew that many would use that freedom to choose what was wrong.

Why do you suppose He took such a risk? After God had created the earth and all of the plants and animals, He looked at His creation and knew that something was missing. He wanted someone that could relate to Him, love Him and bring Him pleasure, not because they were programmed to do so, but because they chose to. He didn't want a robot. He wanted someone who would choose to love Him for who He was. He created man and woman, His highest achievement, and gave them a free will, knowing that they would often make the wrong choices. And as all powerful as God is, He will never interfere with that free will. He will even allow us to go to the pit of hell before He will superimpose His will upon ours. He doesn't want our "have to", He wants our "want to".

All parents want their children to be obedient. But how much more joy it would bring if, instead of just being obedient, they actually wanted to do the things that would please us. If I were to ask my son to take out the trash and he did it without question or complaint, that would make me happy. But what if he simply came to me and said, "Dad, let me take the trash out for you today?" How much more joy I would feel when he did it just because he wanted to please me. That's what God wants of His children. His greatest desire is for us to want to please Him.

All of the other religions of the world, and sadly some Christians, try to find God through head knowledge, through their own intellect. But God wants a heart-to-heart relationship with His people. Think of all the religious people during Jesus' time -- the Pharisees, the Sadducees and the scribes. They had all kinds of religious head-knowledge about God, but it was their hearts He wanted. When we know the heart of God, we understand that He wants to have a true heart-to-heart relationship with each of us. And when we reach this heart-to-heart relationship, we will no longer feel we have to search the scriptures and line them all up to prove what God wants. Nor will we be so likely to say, "All right, God, Your Word promises such and such. Now where is it?" **We will know what He wants because our hearts will be in perfect alignment with His**. It is the privilege of man alone to know the heart of God.

Going back to our Genesis text, we see that God was grieved. He was sorry He had made man in the first place. What can we learn about God from these verses? First, we see that He can be grieved and feel pain. He allows us to bring Him grief and pain while we seek our own pleasure. Second, we see that God really does have a heart. That's not just a little cliche we use so that we can talk about the heart of God. The Bible tells us that God has a heart and He can feel pain in His heart, just as we can. In fact, He not only feels His own pain, He feels our pain as well. Any parent knows the pain that is felt when his children are in pain. God, in the same way, feels the pain of His children.

Why is it that man so often rebels against God? Why does there seem to be so much evil in his heart? For the answer, we must go back to the first man, to the Garden of Eden. Now understand, man's first sin had nothing to do with God trying to deprive him of a piece of fruit. Rather, God wanted man to have no knowledge of sin. He had created him for perfect fellowship and never intended him to know anything about evil. That's why He forbade him to eat of that one tree in the garden, the tree of the **knowledge** of good and evil. God intended man to simply trust, love and relate to Him, not to be faced with making his own choices of what is right or wrong. He intended for him to know and experience only good.

God also provided a tree of life and a beautiful garden from which man could eat and enjoy. Just think about it for a minute. If we did not know evil, what a pure relationship we would have with God -- what perfect peace. However, because the first human beings chose to disobey God in an attempt to become like Him, we now have to continually make a choice between right and wrong, good and evil. It is this whole issue of choice that relates to the heart of God. It's our choice. God's heart was filled with pain because man made the wrong choices.

Now let's go to Jeremiah 17. In verse 9 we read, *"The heart is more deceitful than all else and is desperately sick; who can understand it?"* What a picture of man's heart -- so sick and wicked that no one can understand it. No wonder God's heart is grieved.

Psalm 44:21 asks, *"would not God have discovered it, since he knows the secrets of the heart?"* We can hide behind a beautiful facade as far as man is concerned, but God sees what is in our heart. We can't hide anything from Him. He knows our thoughts, our intentions, everything hidden within us. We can hide from man, but not from God. This is why it is so important that we know God's heart.

In the 23rd chapter of 2nd Samuel we find David and his "mighty men" fighting with the Philistines. The Philistines were camped in Bethlehem, while David and his men were camped in a stronghold outside of the city. Tired and thirsty, David says in the 15th verse, *"Oh, that someone would get me a drink of water from the well near the gate of Bethlehem!"* Note, David wasn't giving anyone an order to risk their lives to get him the water. He was simply making a casual statement. But look what happened. Three of his men slipped out of camp, broke through the camp of the Philistines and got David some water from the well. No one told them to go; they did it on their own. Why? Why did they risk their lives to get a drink of water for David? It was out of pure devotion to him. They were motivated by love. Their hearts were with their king and they were willing to risk their lives for him. This is the kind of devotion that God is looking for in all of us. He wants us to be willing to risk everything we have, even our own lives, for Him. There wasn't anything spiritual about what these men did for David. They just loved him. That's what God wants of us. That is the **HEART OF GOD**.

Note what David did with the water. Did he drink it and tell the men how great it was? No. He simply poured it out on the ground as an offering to the Lord. I was sharing this story with a church one morning and that's about as far as I had planned to go with it. But God spoke to my heart and said, "Is it okay if I spill your ministry out on the ground like that?" Wow! I had been teaching about heart motivation and now the Lord was questioning mine. I had to look closely into my own heart. I had been part of a number of ministries starting in Russia and other places, and I wanted to see how they were going to come out. Was I willing to give all of this up if God asked me to? He wants our hearts, not our ministry; but it is only when we have the right heart motivation, that God can really use our ministries.

God gave man the free will to choose, and because of the wrong choices he made, it has become natural for man's heart to be proud and evil. If we are going to serve God, bringing pleasure to Him, we must have a change of heart. It must become our natural desire to choose that which is pleasing to God. We have to get all of the old nature out of our hearts and replace it with the things of God.

The Bible has a lot to say about the heart, both the heart of man and the heart of God. But how can we find the heart of God? How can we please Him? I believe the Bible gives us nine basic keys to the heart of God, nine ways to reach His heart. The next nine chapters will deal with these keys one at a time; but as an introduction, let me simply list them here. The way to God's heart is that we:

1. Have the right heart motivation

2. Understand the fear, the reverence, of God

3. Have whole- hearted commitment

4. Discover the power in unity

5. Develop genuine relationships

6. Walk in humility - put off pride

7. Seek and discern the kingdom of God

8. Desire obedience from the heart

9. Take Jesus' final instructions seriously

These are the ways in which we can reach right into God's heart. And what is to be the outcome of reaching His heart? I believe it is revival, personal revival and revival of the Body of Christ. We will look at this result in more detail in the closing chapter, but for now, let's try to get an understanding of each of these fundamental principles.

CHAPTER 2

THE RIGHT HEART MOTIVATION

"For the eyes of the Lord move to and fro throughout the earth that He may strongly support those whose heart is completely His."
2 Chronicles 16:9 NAS

In 1974, we were traveling to Indonesia where I was doing a film called "Outpouring in Indonesia" for the Assemblies of God Missions Department. We were flying in over the islands and the pilot invited me to come up into the cockpit to take pictures while we landed. In those days they would let you do that, and it would give me just the right shot for introducing the

Island of Ambon. As I sat there, I became fascinated with the little radar in front of me. Its beam kept sweeping back and forth, showing all those little islands. Indonesia is made up of many islands much like the Philippines. The picture of that radar beam stuck in my mind and as I read this scripture I could see God's eyes going back and forth across the earth just like that radar beam. I could almost hear Him saying, "There's a blip. There's another. They're the ones whose hearts are perfect towards Me." That is the way God is looking for us if we have the **RIGHT HEART MOTIVATION**.

2 Chronicles 16:9 is my favorite scripture. Look closely at what it says. God is looking all over the earth for those whose hearts are completely His, or as some other translations put it, whose hearts are perfect for Him. He is looking for those with the right heart motivation. And what does He say that He will do for them? He will *"strongly support"* them. Most of us have been taught somewhere along the line that we must seek God. We are to be the seekers. But this scripture also says God is seeking us, if our heart is right, just as much as we are seeking Him. This is liberating. He is scanning the whole earth for those who are His, so that He can strongly support them.

Now if God is looking for a heart that is perfect, we may ask, how can I be perfect? The Bible says, *"Be perfect, therefore, as your heavenly Father is perfect."* (Matthew 5:48) This sounds like a big order. I believe we get hung up here because we start thinking right away about a performance. But I don't believe that is what He is looking for. I think God is looking more at our attitude. For example, let's look at the lives of David and Peter. David committed adultery and was a party to murder. Peter denied the Lord three times. If it were up to us, we would probably have put them both out of the church. But who did God refer to as "a man after My own heart?" It was David. And who did He pick to preach the first sermon on the day of Pentecost, where 3000 souls were saved? It was old foot-in-mouth Peter, even though he blew it time after time. They both messed up and were far from perfect in their performance, yet God saw their hearts and chose them for great exploits, things for which they will be remembered forever. So it's not just what we do, but why we do it that seems to count with God. You may feel that you have blown it too, but God isn't looking at that. Rather, he is looking at the motivation of your heart.

God wants a pure heart. We may make a mistake now and then and He may have to help us make a mid-course correction, but if our heart is right, we will be pleasing to Him. We are like an airplane that is on automatic pilot. When the wind blows, it may drift a little off course. The crew will have to make occasional mid-course corrections to keep it heading for its intended destination. They don't reject the autopilot, however, just because the wind blows it a little off course now and then.

In the first chapter we saw in Genesis 6:5-6 that when God looked at the sins of man, He was sorry that He had created him. We saw from this scripture that God has a heart, a heart that can be grieved and feel pain, and that man has a heart that can be full of evil. Now let's look a little further at the heart of man. In Jeremiah 17:9 we read, *"The heart is deceitful above all things and beyond cure. Who can understand it?"* In the natural, our heart is deceitful. We think we understand it, but we don't.

We must search our motives for everything we do, even for what we do "for God." Ask yourself, why am I really doing this? Is it because I want to serve God or is it for the way it will make others look at me? Am I doing this for Him or for me? If we are really honest with ourselves, we will often have to admit that there is a little of both involved. God knows. He sees our heart and understands our true motives, even better than we do ourselves.

We must search our own hearts. If we don't, God will. In Psalm 81:12, God said, "*So I gave them over to their stubborn hearts to follow their own devices.*" Proverbs 5:12 speaks of a heart that "*spurned correction*". Our hearts are stubborn and they spurn reproof. God sees what is in every heart! What does He see in yours?

Proverbs 17:3 says that God tests the heart, and in verse 18:12 it says, "*Before his downfall a man's heart is proud.*" In other words, pride of the heart leads to destruction.

The prophet Joel tells us to return to God with all our heart.

> "*Even now,*" declares the LORD, "*return to me with all your heart, with fasting and weeping and mourning.*" Rend your heart and not your garments. Return to the LORD your God, for he is gracious and compassionate, slow to anger and abounding in love, and he relents from sending calamity. Joel 2:12-13

If we turn to God and "rend" our heart, He will not send calamity. The Jewish people used to rend (tear) their clothes as an outward sign of repentance;

but God wants us to rend our hearts, to show Him that our repentance is truly coming from within.

In the sixteenth chapter of First Samuel we find Samuel looking for the one God wants him to anoint as king to replace Saul. He has just seen Eliab, Jesse's oldest son and is sure that this handsome young man must be the one. But God tells him:

> *"Do not consider his appearance or his height, for I have rejected him. The LORD does not look at the things man looks at. Man looks at the outward appearance, but the LORD looks at the heart."* 1 Samuel 16:7

In our relationships we have the same tendency as Samuel -- being attracted to the good looking, handsome types. We look to the preacher on TV that seems to have it all together in looks, speech and the size of his following. When we visit a new church or ministry, we look at the leader's appearance. If he isn't what we expect, we say to ourselves, "Oh boy, he can't be anointed. He doesn't look right."

We also tend to judge the Body of Christ in this way. Then when something happens and our "Mr. Wonderful" falls, we wonder how it could have happened. He had it all together. How could he fall? But that isn't what God looks for. He looks at the heart. He knows everything about us, but He looks at our heart attitude. It isn't how we look or what we do, but our motivation for doing it. His desire is that we have a heart that is perfect toward Him.

As we saw earlier in Psalm 44:21, God knows the secrets of the heart. We can't hide anything from Him.

He knows it all. David found this out and it caused him a real problem. In Psalm 81:12 we read, "*So I* [God] *gave them over to their stubborn hearts...*" God will just let go and let us have our own way when we have a stubborn heart. David talks a lot about the heart in the Psalms. He isn't talking about the muscle that pumps our blood. He is talking about the innermost part of our being, where our thoughts, desires and will reside. This is where we live.

In Proverbs 5:12 King Solomon said, "*How my heart spurned correction!*" We don't want to be corrected, especially by someone else in the Body, or even by God Himself. We may become real spiritual and pray, "O God, cleanse me." But when He does it we cry, "O no, Lord, not that."

Look now at Proverbs 6. Here God is telling us what He hates.

> *There are six things the LORD hates, seven that are detestable to him: haughty eyes, a lying tongue, hands that shed innocent blood, a heart that devises wicked schemes, feet that are quick to rush into evil, a false witness who pours out lies and a man who stirs up dissension among brothers.* (Proverbs 6:16-19)

These are things that really affect our lives. Note, this listing of the things God hates never mentions sexual sins, alcohol or drugs. Rather, it lists sins of the heart. What is first on the list? Haughty eyes. This refers to pride, one of man's most prevalent problems. Pride has been one of the most common causes of ministry failure. God hates pride.

Next on the list is lying. God can't stand lies. We must never lie or exaggerate, even if we think we are helping God by doing so. God wants an honest and open heart. Many of us, especially those of the younger generation, have never been taught real honesty. We don't know how to be honest.

God's love of man makes Him hate hands that shed innocent blood, and a heart that devises wicked plans. These are the murderers and those who always try to stir up trouble. He then speaks of those who run to evil, who just can't stay away from it, and the one who is a false witness (the gossip who testifies falsely against his neighbor). These are all hated by God.

Note that this scripture said there were six thing God hates and seven which are detestable to Him. We have seen the six He hates, now what was the seventh one? What is it that is detestable to God? It is not a **thing** like the first six. It is a **person**. This is the only place I can recall, where God says He hates a man. He says that the one who spreads strife among brothers is detestable to Him. He can't stand the person that causes problems among other believers. There are always those in the church that bring up this and that about someone else, and seek to get every little problem corrected. This is the devil's favorite tool. God is warning that the strife it stirs up is much worse than the problem they were trying to get corrected. We need to learn to let God do the correcting. We must be very careful. These are all issues of the heart. It is wrong heart motivation that God hates.

Now let us look at right heart motivations, the things that God wants in us. Actually, we need a heart transplant. That is why we ask Jesus to come into our heart. We need our heart to be indwelt by His. This is the only way we will find the true heart of God. When we get the motivations of our heart worked out and in order, then the devil won't be able to get a foothold.

David was a man who understood the heart of God. He talked more about it than anyone else in scripture. We can therefore go to the Psalms for a picture of God's desires for man's heart. The people of Israel had the Law and the Ten Commandments, but they were never able to follow them. Most just didn't have the right heart motivation. Jesus Himself chastised them for binding people up in the law while their own hearts were evil within them. As we study the Psalms, we can watch as David's own heart motivations grow and mature. David did some terrible things, yet God said that David was a man after His own heart. How can we reconcile this? In Psalm 15 we read:

> LORD, who may dwell in your sanctuary?
> Who may live on your holy hill? He whose
> walk is blameless and who does what is
> righteous, who speaks the truth from his heart.
> Psalm 15:1-2

What is David asking in verse one? He is questioning how anyone is able to come into God's presence with all the "junk" we have in us. Then in Verse Two he gives us the answer. First he mentions those who walk with integrity and work righteousness. We can all relate with that. We know that is what God wants, men of integrity and righteousness. But then look what comes next. He says, "*and speaks truth in his heart.*" David seems to understand that the problems began or originated in the heart. God is looking for honesty from the heart. Honesty must be our motivation. Our hearts must be real, not "plastic."

Most of us are familiar with Psalm 19 verse 14 which says, "*May the words of my mouth and the meditation of my heart be pleasing in your sight...*" Here David seems to be speaking of a further step. He is concerned not just about the words he speaks, but also about his meditations, his thoughts. He wants even his thought life to be pleasing to God. Look at what lust, the lust for sexual pleasure, for money, for power, for food and drink, has done to our thought life today. Many Christians, even some leaders, are addicted to pornography or are under some other bondage. But it doesn't have to be an addiction to be a problem. It can be very subtle. What do we see on TV every day? So called "family shows" are full of sexual innuendoes and situations that feed our worldly appetites. In fact, even the commercials play on our lustful desires. But God wants even our thought life to be pure and pleasing to Him.

Go next to Psalm 24.

Who may ascend the hill of the LORD? Who may stand in his holy place? He who has clean hands and a pure heart... Psalm 24:3-4

Again David is seeing God's desire for a pure heart. He asks who is able to approach God, or who is able to get to where God wants him. Then, finding the answer, he declares that it is he who has clean hands and a pure heart. David is now beginning to get the picture.

In Psalm 32:11b he says, "*...sing, all you who are*

upright in heart!" And in Psalm 37:31 David, in speaking of the characteristics of a righteous man, says, *"The law of his God is in his heart; his feet do not slip."* It is important to understand when the Law or Word of God is in your heart you aren't going to get into much trouble. God's Word in our head won't do us a lot of good, but God's Word in our heart will be our protection. In fact, when we have God's Word implanted in our hearts, we will take pleasure in doing His will. Psalm 40:8 says, *"I desire to do your will, O my God; your law is within my heart."*

As we said before, this is the place God wants us to be. He wants our "want to" and when His Word or law is in our heart, we will want to do His will. Then in Verse 10 David goes on to say that he is not hiding these things he is discovering in his heart. He is beginning to share and proclaim them.

As David began to realize how important his heart was to God, he was able to turn to God and seek a cleansing of his heart. We see this in Psalm 51, which was written after his sin with Bathsheba:

> *Create in me a pure heart, O God, and renew a steadfast spirit within me. Do not cast me from your presence or take your Holy Spirit from me. Restore to me the joy of your salvation and grant me a willing spirit, to sustain me.* Psalm 51:10-12

God must have smiled when He heard David cry out like this. He must have said to Himself, "Wow, My son David has almost got it now." This was a beautiful heart cry of David, but there is still something missing. Do we see what it is? David is asking God to do it all.

He just wants to push God's button and have Him fix everything. I remember years ago in the Sears catalogs that each product line had a Good, a Better, and a Best. Like these Sears' products, this is a **good** prayer, but let's turn to Psalm 139 and see the **best**. Remember, God doesn't want good, He wants the best. Here David prays:

> *Search me, O God, and know my heart; test me and know my anxious thoughts. See if there is any offensive way in me, and lead me in the way everlasting.* Psalm 139:23-24

Notice that this time David isn't asking God to do it all for him. He asks Him to search his heart and to test him to see if there is anything else he has to get rid of. Wow! I think I have enough tests, yet David asks for more. Then he asks God to lead him -- not to do everything for him, but to lead him. This was the attitude of David that likely made God smile and say, "Now this is a man after My own heart." This is the attitude that motivates God to action. It is what we are inside, not what we do, that God is looking at. David asked God to test him. Do we dare say to God, "Test me"? We had better be careful, as He might do just that. David learned that he had to get all that was not of God out of his heart. Then he could ask God to lead him and he knew that He would do it, and that he would be able to follow. **GOD IS MORE MOTIVATED BY WHAT WE ARE THAN BY WHAT WE DO!**

Jesus also spoke a lot about the heart. "*Blessed are the pure in heart, for they will see God.*" (Matthew 5:8) Many think that this means that we will see God when we go to heaven, but I believe that if we have a pure heart we can see Him right here on earth. We may not see Him physically, but we can still see Him. We can see Him in many aspects of His creation, in a beautiful scene, in a beautiful sky, in the lives of His people.

Some years ago, we were taking Bibles into China. We had a meeting with some of the believers in a small hotel room. As we met secretly in that tiny room, there was a beautiful little Chinese woman sitting there. It was not that she was physically beautiful or anything like that, but there was such a glow about her that it looked like she had a light around her. As I started talking to her, I was humbled by her presence. I could see God in this lovely Chinese lady. Here we were bringing Bibles in and thinking we had it all together, but as we talked with the believers there, we found that there was already a great revival going on in China. God is there and His presence is being manifested.

Prior to going to China, we had just come from the Philippines, where I had had great success teaching in seminars. As we were coming back on the train from Canton, I started saying to the Lord, "Oh, if I could only be teaching in this country too. They are so open to Your Word." Then the Holy Spirit said something that shocked me. He said, "I am raising up a church in China without spot or wrinkle, and I don't want it polluted with western ideologies." Now in the natural that would seem quite a put-down to a missionary, but not really. It is God's timing, His way. The next time we went in, we were happy just to take the Bibles.

I go to many countries to teach, but I never go without also learning from those I teach. Just the commitment I see in people who are hungry for God is an education in itself. We are so spoiled in America. It is hard to just get us to church on Sunday, yet the people in the Philippines will walk two to three days to go to a meeting and hear the Word. They will hitch hike on the back of trucks and sleep on the side of the road or come in small boats just to get there. They are hungry for God. I've seen people on the Mosquito Coast of Honduras who would crowd into a little tin-roofed church, in pouring rain, with the wind ripping part of the roof off. They would be soaked to the skin but they would stay to hear the Word of God. I was the preacher, yet I was humbled by their hunger for God. The right heart motivation creates in us a real hunger for God.

As He was teaching His disciples in His Sermon on the Mount, Jesus warned them about laying up their treasures on earth. He then said, *"For where your treasure is, there your heart will be also."* (Matthew 6:21) What is the motivation of our hearts? What do we treasure, or what is our goal? Where do we spend our time? What are we working for? Are we working at our jobs just to make money? What is the money for? Is it for the Lord's work or is it so that we can have things better for ourselves? These are the questions that reveal our true heart motivation. And what is it that is drawing us away from God? Is it family? Job? Even our ministry can draw us away from a heart relationship with God. God wants us, not what we are doing. When He gets us, we will do the right things because we love Him.

"For out of the overflow of the heart the mouth speaks." (Matthew 12:34b) What is coming out of our mouths? Are we cursing or blessing? Are we complaining or rejoicing? Jesus said of the Pharisees, *"These people honor me with their lips, but their hearts are far from me."* (Matthew 15:8) Might He be saying this of the Body of Christ today? In 1 John 3:18 we read, *"Dear*

children, let us not love with words or tongue but with actions and in truth." God is looking for more than lip service. Again, in Luke 16:15, Jesus says to the Pharisees, *"You are the ones who justify yourselves in the eyes of men, but God knows your hearts. What is highly valued among men is detestable in God's sight."* The Pharisees were always trying to justify themselves to the people, but God knew their hearts. We have to be careful of what we think is important to God.

The tenth chapter of Romans says:

*That if you confess with your mouth, "Jesus is Lord," and **believe in your heart** that God raised him from the dead, you will be saved. For it is **with your heart** that you believe and are justified, and it is with your mouth that you confess and are saved.* Romans 10:9-10 (emphasis added)

In our salvation experience we understand that it is "in the heart" that man believes. We must be careful, therefore, when we lead someone to the Lord, that it isn't just a head experience. In Russia, we had to spend a lot of time on this with those who came forward. They were to be new creatures, old things had to pass away. It was essential for them to understand this.

We find in Philippians 4:

And the peace of God, which transcends all understanding, will guard your hearts and your minds in Christ Jesus. Philippians 4:7

We are to guard our hearts and minds. What are we watching on television? What are we reading? What are we listening to? Gossip? Negative talk? Put downs? Are we guarding our hearts and minds from the ungodly things of this world? How do we know what is truly ruling our hearts? The book of Hebrews says:

> *For the word of God is living and active. Sharper than any double-edged sword, it penetrates even to dividing soul and spirit, joints and marrow; **it judges the thoughts and attitudes of the heart.*** Hebrews 4:12 (emphasis added)

How do we know the state of our heart? Judge it by the Word of God. That is the standard. I can't overemphasize the importance of sincerity, of being real. It is so important in our relationship with God and with others. We must be real to be a part of the kingdom of God. Our desire to be real with God determines our destiny in His kingdom. This must be our heart motivation.

CHAPTER 3

UNDERSTANDING THE FEAR OF GOD

*Our Father in heaven, hallowed
be your name,*

Matthew 6:9

We are of course very familiar with this first line
from what we call the Lord's prayer. But how many
times have we prayed it without thinking about what we
were saying? For that matter, do we really understand
what we are praying? What does it mean for God's name
to be hallowed? The dictionary defines "hallowed" as,
"to make or honor as holy." I believe, however, that
there is much more to it as used here by the Lord. I
believe that it is more than even a holy awareness of

who God is.

In another translation of the Bible, this text reads *"feared be Thy name."* I will admit that this bothered me at first. Like so many, my early knowledge of God was to be afraid of Him. I didn't even like to read the Old Testament because I saw so much about the fear, and even the wrath of God. As a Christian, I felt that I had been set free of such fear. I no longer believed that if I wasn't good God was going to zap me, yet when I saw so much about the fear of God in the Old Testament, I avoided it.

Even before I knew anything about God, the enemy somehow got it into me that God was somewhere up in the sky just waiting for me to make a mistake. As a child, I was raised in New Jersey, near the Lakehurst Naval Air Station, where they kept a fleet of huge blimps. At that time they used blimps to search for submarines; they would practice all day trying to sneak up on them. Sometimes I would be out in the yard playing and suddenly look up and see one of these huge things hovering right over my head. It would frighten me because someone had told me that Santa was up there watching to see if I was good enough to get anything for Christmas. Later, when I outgrew Santa Claus, I somehow transposed God for Santa and felt that He was up there watching for me to make a mistake. This made me afraid of God at a very early age.

I have spent more than 25 years of my life as a professional photographer. Much of my early mission work was doing film documentaries of mission works all over the world. Drawing on this photographic experience for an example while I was ministering in Africa, I was sharing with the people about having an out-of-focus picture of God. While I thought I was teaching them, the Holy Spirit prompted me and said, "That's for you, son." Then He showed me that I too had an out-of-focus picture of God. I had an unhealthy fear of Him and felt that if I didn't do everything just right, He was going to punish me in some way. I even felt that I might somehow miss heaven if I didn't do everything right to please Him. Whenever I would try to read the Old Testament, or even the New Testament, it would just increase this attitude, since all I would see was the fear of God. I didn't understand what it really meant to fear God.

This attitude continued until some years ago while we were in the Philippines, and all of our meetings were canceled for the week. The Lord impressed on me to use this time to read the Old Testament. This was not just a time to read through it, but a time for real study. As I read morning noon and night, God showed me that the fear of God is not to be afraid of Him, but to have the respectful awareness of who He is. **The fear of God is the sense of awe and reverence of all His holiness**. If we can get this kind of fear into our hearts and spirits, we will never have a problem doing what God asks us to do. When we know who God is, we won't have a problem trusting Him or being in the plan He has for our lives.

As God's children, we have no reason to be afraid of Him. It's only when we knowingly go against His will that we have a reason to fear His wrath. There are many places in both the Old and New Testaments that say "fear not." Here the Old Testament uses the Hebrew word "yare" (yaw-ray') for fear and the New Testament uses the Greek word "phobeo" (fob-eh'-o). Both mean to frighten or make afraid. This is the wrong kind of fear. Fear should not make us afraid of God; rather it should give us a proper respect for Him.

God has set up a series of laws to govern our lives that are just as sure as the law of gravity. If we drop a book, it will fall to the floor. If we disobey what God is telling us to do, it will adversely affect our lives. We need not be afraid of God but we should fear the consequences of our wrong actions. The proper fear of God leads us into the desire to be obedient. It's not that God wants to take anything away from us. He doesn't even want us to settle for what is good, when we can have the best.

The proper fear of God leads to obedience, not because we have to, but because we want to. When we first got saved, we had the attitude that if we didn't do right we would go to hell. While there is some truth in this, it isn't a very good foundation on which to build a relationship with God. We do right because we want to. We are thankful that He has made a way for us to come to Him and be cleansed of our past. This is the relationship He is looking for in us, that we come to Him out of our own desire to please Him.

Psalm 2:11 says that we are to "*Serve the LORD with fear and rejoice with trembling.*" This is not being afraid of Him. That kind of fear does not make us rejoice. We will be joyful, however, when we worship and serve Him with reverence, with an awesome respect for who He is.

> *Oh, that their hearts would be inclined to fear me and keep all my commands always, so that it might go well with them and their children forever!* Deuteronomy 5:29

Note, God is after our hearts. He doesn't just want our mental assent, He wants our hearts. This is a principle He wants us to understand about our fear of Him. He wants our hearts to fear, not be afraid, but have the deep respect and knowledge of who He is. God doesn't want us to be afraid of Him; He invites us to come boldly to the throne of grace (Hebrews 4:16). We know that we can't just go out and do whatever we want or push a button and have God do it for us. He is the God of the Universe, the Creator of everything we have or see. We are to let God be God and be in awe of Him. This is the principle of the fear of God.

Now let's look at the blessings associated with this proper fear. Why does this scripture say that we should fear God? It is *"that it might go well with them and their children forever."* It is not that God wants our fear just for His own benefit; He wants it for our good because He, our Creator, knows what is best for us.

Turn now to the first chapter of Proverbs. In verse seven we read, *"The fear of the LORD is the beginning of knowledge."* Then in the ninth chapter we read in the tenth verse, *"The fear of the LORD is the beginning of wisdom,"* a statement that is repeated in Psalm 111:10. I think we all know what knowledge is, but how about wisdom? Wisdom is the ability to use the knowledge we have in the right way. So, the fear of the Lord not only leads to knowledge, it teaches us how to put that knowledge to its best use.

The world is full of knowledge. We know how to make computers and how to send men to the moon, but we seldom have the wisdom to foster right relationships or properly raise our families. Do you see the difference? Knowledge can come from many sources, but wisdom comes from God. Think back to the fall of man. What were Adam and Eve seeking? They were looking for the **knowledge** of good and evil, knowledge that they would not know how to use. If man had obeyed and let God have His heart's desire, we would never have had to know evil. But once we knew it, the doors were opened wide, and we dashed right in. If there is one thing I really desire from God it is wisdom. Without it, all of the knowledge in the world is of little value.

There are many more promises in the Bible related to the fear of the Lord. In the fourteenth chapter of Proverbs we read:

> *In the fear of the Lord there is strong confidence, and his children will have refuge. The fear of the Lord is a fountain of life, that one may avoid the snares of death.* Proverbs 14:26-27 NAS

These verses speak of the fear of the Lord as being a "*strong confidence*" and a "*refuge*" for the children. Some translations make this a "*strong fortress*" or a place of protection. In either case, the Bible speaks of the fear of the Lord in terms of protection; we are protected by our fear of God. Then in verse 27 we see that fear is a "*fountain of life*", the place from where all life comes. Without the fear of God, we don't really have life. We may be alive, but not really living.

Look next at Proverbs 22.

> *Humility and the fear of the LORD bring wealth and honor and life.* Proverbs 22:4

It's interesting how the Bible ties the fear of the Lord in with other principles. Here, we see it tied in with humility. It says that both humility and the fear of the Lord have their reward in *"wealth and honor and life"*. You see, God can trust us with wealth only when we properly fear Him. He knows that if we fear Him we are not going to destroy ourselves. Without God, many people are destroyed by wealth. We can say the same thing about honor, because without the fear of God we don't know how to handle honor either. People start saying someone is a great teacher or a great preacher, and without a healthy fear of God, the praise will go to his head. Just look at how many "great" men in ministry have fallen. I believe there would be no so called "fall from grace" if they had a genuine fear of God. When we really understand who God is, we don't want to do wrong. The fear of God will bring us true honor, not just our name in lights.

Psalm 19:9 says, *"The fear of the LORD is pure, enduring forever.."* The fear of the Lord is so clean and pure that it is everlasting. There is an enduring value in the fear of the Lord. Again, this is not being afraid of God, but rather being in awe of Him. Then in Verse 10 it goes on to say that this fear is *"more precious than gold"* and *"sweeter than honey."* It is better than anything else.

The 25th Psalm says:

Who, then, is the man that fears the LORD? He will instruct him in the way chosen for him. He will spend his days in prosperity, and his descendants will inherit the land. The LORD confides in those who fear him; he makes his covenant known to them. Psalm 25:12-14

These are some powerful promises for those who fear God. God's instruction is a precious commodity these days, but here we read that He will instruct us in what we should do. Do we want God's instruction? With Him instructing us, we can be sure that we will be going in the right direction. Scripture then says of the one who fears God, "*He will spend his days in prosperity.*" When we fear God, He can trust us with prosperity. Now prosperity doesn't necessarily mean monetary wealth. Prosperity may also refer to our being blessed in other ways. And His Word goes on to include our descendants in this prosperity. We often read and hear about blessings, but do we really know what it means to be blessed? I think being blessed can best be defined as **being ultimately fulfilled and deeply satisfied**.

Verse 14 of this text tells us that the Lord will confide in us, reveal His secrets to us and let us know His covenant. Think of it. The God of Heaven will confide in us! He will let us know and understand all of the little secret things hidden in His Word. This is a rich promise. To think that at one time I didn't even want to read the Old Testament, and now I find that God is just waiting to reveal all of His secrets to me. There is real freedom in this promise. We no longer need to be bound up by the devil or with the traditions of man. We are free to know the secret heart of God, if we have the proper reverence for Him. The heart of God is reaching out to touch the world to build a family, and God wants a large family.

Reading on in the Psalms, the promises get better and better. In Psalm 31 we read:

> *How great is your goodness, which you have stored up for those who fear you, which you*

bestow in the sight of men on those who take refuge in you. Psalm 31:19

If we fear the Lord and take refuge in Him, we will experience God's goodness, the good things that He has for His own. What more could we ask for than the goodness of God? And then Verse 20 tells us that He will keep us safe from the conspiracies of man and the strife of tongues. That is powerful!

Recently, as we were traveling by train to Volgograd in the plains area of Russia, I saw these huge square grain elevators that seemed to be out in the middle of nowhere. I didn't know what they were at first, as I was used to seeing ours which are round. Someone had to tell me that they were used to store grain. Looking at these huge buildings full of grain reminded me of this scripture and how God has so many good things stored up for those who fear Him. All I could say was WOW! *"How great is your goodness, which you have stored up for those who fear you."*

In the 33rd Psalm we have another great promise for those who fear the Lord..

But the eyes of the LORD are on those who fear him, on those whose hope is in his unfailing love, to deliver them from death and keep them alive in famine. Psalm 33:18-19

When we fear God, He will be watching out for us. If the eyes of the Lord are on us, we are well covered and protected. If we fear Him and our hope is in His lovingkindness, we know that we can trust Him to deliver us from death and from famine.

God let me see this promise in action as we were coming in for a landing in Honduras. The plane suddenly started dropping, the stall warning was sounding, and all I could see was the ground coming up fast. We had been caught in a down-draft coming over a mountain and I knew that there was no way that we were going to make it to the runway. This was the closest I had ever come to death, and I was sure it was all over. If I had been on the wing, I could have reached out and grabbed a handful of leaves. I was making my peace with God, as we skimmed over the trees. As we landed safely at the airport, God showed me that there were two hands on the airplane, one holding it up and the other pulling it down. God's hand was the strongest. He delivers those who fear Him, even from death.

This is reinforced again in Psalm 34:7 which promises, *"The angel of the LORD encamps around those who fear him, and he delivers them.."* Think about it. If we fear God, we have His angels encamped around us. I know that this is true. About fifteen years ago, we were in Jamaica. We were in an old English car, coming down a hill, when the brakes gave out completely. This was on one of the main streets in downtown Kingston. There was a bus in front of us, cars coming from the other direction, and no place for us to go. We were only traveling about 30 to 35 miles per hour, but with no brakes, there was going to be a serious impact if we slammed into the rear of the bus. Our driver tried to swerve onto the sidewalk to lessen the impact.

Now don't ask me to explain what happened; but instantaneously, in the blink of an eye, that car, my wife and I, the driver and all our camera equipment were translated two and a half blocks down the street and were coasting to a stop in an alley. I went back and looked over the situation and there was no way that we could have gotten out of it. To this day, I believe that God's angels delivered us. I don't know if we went through, over or around that bus, but we were delivered. If we fear the Lord, He will deliver us; He does have His angels encamped around us.

A little further on in Psalm 34 we read:

Fear the LORD, you his saints, for those who fear him lack nothing. The lions may grow weak and hungry, but those who seek the LORD lack no good thing. Psalm 34:9-10

Do we realize what God is saying? If we fear the Lord, we will lack no good thing; we will have all of our needs fulfilled. The animals may feel hunger, but His saints will lack nothing. Are you a saint? If you love and fear God, and desire His heart, you are. A saint is someone who is set apart for God. He is one who knows the fear of God.

The Psalms are so full of God's promises to those who fear Him. Chapter 103 says:

For as high as the heavens are above the earth, so great is his love for those who fear him; as far as the east is from the west, so far has he removed our transgressions from us. As a father has compassion on his children, so the LORD has compassion on those who fear him; Psalm 103:11-13

How far are the heavens above the earth? How far is the east from the west? This is how great God's love is toward those who fear Him. It is without measure. We must remember, David wrote this long before Christ was born, long before the New Covenant, the Covenant of Grace. Yet look at what it says. It promises that if we fear the Lord, He will remove our transgressions from us by as far as the east is from the west.

The 13th verse speaks of compassion. We don't hear much about compassion any more, but if you want to see miracles, show compassion. Just look through the four gospels in the New Testament. Almost every time Jesus healed someone, it says first that He had compassion on them. It was through His compassion that the healings were released. In Matthew 14:4 Jesus had compassion and healed the sick. In Matthew 15:32 He had compassion and fed the 4000, and in Matthew 20:34 He had compassion on the blind men and healed them. In Mark 1:41 we see Jesus healing a leper out of compassion, and in Luke 7:13 He had compassion on a widow and raised her only son from death.

Compassion is a key to ministry. We must understand compassion. Ask the Lord to show you about compassion. It won't be comfortable, because you will have to put yourself in the shoes of those to whom you are ministering. When you have compassion, you cannot be judgmental.

Psalm 112:1 says, "*Praise the LORD. Blessed is the man who fears the LORD, who finds great delight in his commands.*" Remember what we said it meant to be blessed. It is to be ultimately fulfilled and deeply satisfied. This is what is promised for those who fear God. We will even find delight in His commandments. The commands of God are not a hard taskmaster. We find delight in them when we understand the fear of God. Then in verses seven and eight we read, "*He will have no fear of bad news....His heart is secure, he will have no fear....*" (emphasis added). This speaks of the other type of fear, of being afraid. If we fear God with a reverential fear, we will never need to be afraid of man.

There is another great promise in Psalm 147:11 which says, "*the LORD delights in those who fear him.*" Do you want to be favored by God? I know I do. We were created to have fellowship with God. He wants our fellowship and hopes we want His. He wants to give us so much, but we must be in a place where we can safely receive it. If we fear Him, then He will favor us. Proverbs 10:27 says that the fear of God adds length to life. We will even live longer if we fear God.

In Proverbs 3 we see:

Do not be wise in your own eyes; fear the LORD and shun evil. This will bring health to your body and nourishment to your bones. Proverbs 3:7-8

These verses seem to contrast pride with the fear of the Lord. While pride is many times condemned in the Bible as being evil, here we are told that the opposite of pride, the fear of God, will bring us healing and refreshment. And for the ladies, Proverbs 31:30 says, "*Charm is deceptive, and beauty is fleeting; but a woman who fears the LORD is to be praised..*" Do you see what is real? It isn't appearances; it isn't charm and beauty; it is only the fear of the Lord. That is what brings His praise.

Proverbs 8:13 says,"*To fear the LORD is to hate*

evil" and Proverbs 16:6 says, *"through the fear of the LORD a man avoids evil."* If we fear God, we will automatically hate evil, because we will recognize it for what it is. Through such fear, we will avoid evil and the trouble it brings. As missionaries, we have found that we must be especially careful. It is so easy to be caught up in little white lies, for example. When we hold a meeting and there are 70 or 80 in attendance, it is always easy to speak of having about a hundred in the meeting. God doesn't want that; He wants only the truth. We don't have to help Him out by exaggerating.

Now that we have seen the many benefits of having a proper fear of the Lord, how do we cultivate that fear within ourselves? In Proverbs 1 we read:

> *"Then they will call to me but I will not answer; they will look for me but will not find me. Since they hated knowledge and did not choose to fear the LORD,"* Proverbs 1:28-29 (emphasis added)

No one can pray and lay hands on you to receive the fear of God. It is something you have to **choose** for yourself. That's the only way you can receive it. You have to come before God and make a commitment to fear Him. God created every other creature with instinct -- programmed to do what it was intended to do -- but He made man with a free will to choose. God wants us to choose to fear Him. And when we do, we will start to see things happen in our lives that we never knew were possible.

In the first chapter of Malachi, we read a great warning from God about those who don't fear Him. The book of Malachi was the last book of the Old Testament, the last revelation that God gave the people of Israel under the Old Covenant. It was followed by a period of about four hundred years of silence before the birth of Christ. These teachings of Malachi, therefore, seem to be God's final warning to His Old Covenant people.

"A son honors his father, and a servant his master. If I am a father, where is the honor due me? If I am a master, where is the respect due me?" says the LORD Almighty. "It is you, O priests, who show contempt for my name. But you ask, 'How have we shown contempt for your name?' You place defiled food on my altar. But you ask, 'How have we defiled you?' By saying that the Lord's table is contemptible. When you bring blind animals for sacrifice, is that not wrong? When you sacrifice crippled or diseased animals, is that not wrong? Try offering them to your governor! Would he be pleased with you? Would he accept you?" says the LORD Almighty. "Now implore God to be gracious to us. With such offerings from your hands, will he accept you?"--says the LORD Almighty. "Oh, that one of you would shut the temple doors, so that you would not light useless fires on my altar! I am not pleased with you," says the LORD Almighty, "and I will accept no offering from your hands. My name will be great among the nations, from the rising to the setting of the sun. In every place incense and pure offerings will be brought to my name, because my name will be great among the nations," says the LORD Almighty. "But you profane it by saying of the Lord's table, 'It is defiled,' and of its food, 'It

is contemptible.' And you say, 'What a burden!' and you sniff at it contemptuously," says the LORD Almighty. "When you bring injured, crippled or diseased animals and offer them as sacrifices, should I accept them from your hands?" says the LORD. "Cursed is the cheat who has an acceptable male in his flock and vows to give it, but then sacrifices a blemished animal to the Lord. For I am a great king," says the LORD Almighty, "and my name is to be feared among the nations."
Malachi 1:6-14

Perhaps it was because they didn't heed this last warning that there was such a long time of silence before the Lord came. God was saying to them, "Where is the respect, honor and fear due Me, when you sacrifice blemished animals?" They were just giving God their leftovers. I know a missionary couple who were in Cameroon, West Africa. They received a box from their home church and were so excited. They didn't know what was in it, but they still had to pay duty to get it out of Customs. Then when they got home and opened it, it was a whole box of used tea bags. Someone in their church had decided that it would be good to save all their old tea bags and send them to the missionaries. This is the kind of thing that God was warning the people about in Malachi, and it is the kind of thing that, if we fear God, we would neither dare nor want to do. We are to give to God and His work the best, the pure, the unblemished, not the leftovers.

The New Testament speaks often of the fear of God. In the first eleven verses of Acts 5, we are told the story of Ananias and his wife Sapphira, who sold a piece of property and then, when they brought the proceeds to Peter, lied about how much they had gotten for it. Here we are given a warning about giving and not having the proper fear of God. In this case, they were both struck dead. They put greed ahead of their fear of God. They didn't have a real reverence for Him.

In Paul's second letter to the Corinthian church, the first verse of Chapter 7 says, "...*let us purify ourselves from everything that contaminates body and spirit, perfecting holiness out of reverence for God..*" We can cleanse or purify ourselves through the fear of God. It will even perfect our holiness. Then is Acts 9:31 we are told that the church "*enjoyed a time of peace.*" while "*it grew in numbers, living in the fear of the Lord.*" The proper fear of God will bring both peace and growth to the church.

Finally, the whole subject of the fear of God can be summed up with these two verses.

> *Now all has been heard; here is the conclusion of the matter: Fear God and keep his commandments, for this is the whole duty of man. For God will bring every deed into judgment, including every hidden thing, whether it is good or evil.* Ecclesiastes 12:13-14

CHAPTER 4

COMMITMENT - A DECISION

"If anyone comes to me and does not hate his father and mother, his wife and children, his brothers and sisters--yes, even his own life--he cannot be my disciple.

Luke 14:26

Throughout most of the New Testament, Jesus teaches us to love one another. In fact, He even goes so far as to teach us to love our enemies (Luke 6:27). But now, suddenly, He's telling us to "hate" even our own family. How can this be? How could Jesus, of all people, speak of hating anyone? When I first read this, I was ready to give up. I felt that I couldn't do what He was asking. How could I hate my own family to be His disciple?

But what is Jesus really saying? God has always looked for those who were completely sold-out to Him. What Jesus is saying is that compared to our commitment and love for Him, our relationship is to be like hate to the people we love and respect here on earth. That's the kind of commitment and love He wants from us. It's not that we really hate them, but that compared to our love for Him, it is like hate. That is real commitment.

Without this love and commitment, Jesus says that we cannot be His disciples. But just what is a disciple? I like to think of him or her as a "disciplined follower of Jesus." The words disciple and discipline come from the same root. We must be disciplined to be Jesus' disciple. Discipline seems to be a scarce commodity these days. We have taken the freedom God has so graciously given us and used it for our own pleasure, to have our own way. We say we are free, but the only true freedom is our freedom to choose to serve God.

Note also, this scripture says that a disciple must hate even his own life. God dealt with me on this some years ago while my wife and I were serving as leaders for a group of young people. Revival had broken out amongst the youth in a rural town near Parsons, Kansas, in the early 1970's. Over a hundred of these young people had made a commitment to Christ, including about a third of the students in the local High School. Some of these same kids went on to become missionaries themselves; others have continuously supported us in our mission efforts.

It was while I was teaching these young people from this passage in Luke, I said to God, "Father, I would probably be willing to lay down my life for You if necessary. With Your help, I would be willing to say that I was a Christian, even at the risk of being shot." Then the Spirit of the Lord said something really shocking to me. He said, "That would be easy compared to what I am going to ask you to do." When I looked at this scripture again, He seemed to superimpose the word "lifestyle" where it said "life".

Now this made me think; what is my lifestyle? I had a pretty good lifestyle, as many of us do in this Nation. It was better than I had realized before going to other countries and seeing how most of the rest of the world lives. We had a nice home on five acres, which we had designed and built just the way we wanted it. We had two cars in the garage, a good job with security and a pension plan. We felt set for life.

We were not wealthy, but we were comfortable. God, however, wanted to move us out of our comfort zone. We all have comfort zones. It was at this time that God spoke to me about hating my lifestyle and He began dealing with me about it. In addition to our home and job, I had about $3,000 worth of model trains, a lot of camera equipment, and about 13,000 color slides of locomotives and trains. Now you know that this was more than just a little hobby with me. But God was telling me to hate my lifestyle. To make a long story short, within a year we had sold our home, most of the trains and things we didn't really need, put the rest in the back of a U-Haul truck, left Kansas, and headed for Bible training in Texas, singing "I have decided to follow

Jesus. No turning back, no turning back."

In addition to upsetting our own lifestyle, mine and my wife's, we also upset our children's. Our son was just going into high school and our daughter was in high school, where she had made many friends. Needless to say, we were under a lot of pressure. But I knew in my heart, if I was going to really seek God's will in this, I had to "walk the talk." Through this, God has shown us that it is not what we've got, but what's got us that holds us back from Him. Veteran missionary Wayne Meyers has often said, "It's okay to have nice things or to drive a Mercedes, but always keep a For Sale sign in the trunk." God wants us to be fulfilled, but never to put our possessions ahead of Him.

I thought my life's work was to be a cinematographer. That's what I wanted to do, film mission work. Then, while on Mindanao, in the Philippines, God spoke to my heart to lay down my camera and go out and teach His Word. That was in 1983, and that's what we have been doing ever since.

In Luke 18 we read:

"I tell you the truth," Jesus said to them, "no one who has left home or wife or brothers or parents or children for the sake of the kingdom of God will fail to receive many times as much in this age and, in the age to come, eternal life." Luke 18:29-30

No matter what we give up for the Lord, He will give back many times as much. Every time we have given up a home, He has given back to us a better one. We cannot out-give the Lord.

Now remember, we are talking about reaching the heart of God. Commitment is a decision, a decision we have to make. Jesus said that we cannot be His disciples unless we hate our lifestyle and even our families, as compared to our love for Him. But Jesus is always reasonable in what He expects of us. Let's look at Luke 14, beginning with the 28th verse.

> *"Suppose one of you wants to build a tower. Will he not first sit down and estimate the cost to see if he has enough money to complete it? For if he lays the foundation and is not able to finish it, everyone who sees it will ridicule him, saying, 'This fellow began to build and was not able to finish.'"* Luke 14:28-30

Jesus then went on to talk about a king who doesn't count the cost of battle. In verse 33, He says, *"In the same way, any of you who does not give up everything he has cannot be my disciple."* He is saying to us, "Sit down and count the cost." Jesus is always realistic and honest with us. He knows that not everyone will be willing to make this total commitment to become a true disciple. Let's look at what hinders us in making that total commitment.

Turn to Deuteronomy, the 20th chapter, beginning with verse 5. I call these the hindrances to the call of God in our lives. I like to share these with all missionary candidates, as I feel it is important for them to understand what the hindrances may be to their call to serve God in the mission field. This doesn't mean that we may use these as excuses, but we must be realistic about it, as God is realistic. He is raising up an army, and He doesn't want there to be weakness in His army.

Now let's look at this scenario. The Israeli army was up against the enemy, against overwhelming odds. They turned to God and asked Him for help, and here is what He said to them:

> *The officers shall say to the army: "Has anyone built a new house and not dedicated it? Let him go home, or he may die in battle and someone else may dedicate it. Has anyone planted a vineyard and not begun to enjoy it? Let him go home, or he may die in battle and someone else enjoy it. Has anyone become pledged to a woman and not married her? Let him go home, or he may die in battle and someone else marry her." Then the officers shall add, "Is any man afraid or fainthearted? Let him go home so that his brothers will not become disheartened too."*
> Deuteronomy 20:5-8

What is God saying are the hindrances to our discipleship? In verse 5, He speaks of a man who has built a house. What does a house represent? It is a symbol of a man's security. Remember what Jesus told us in Luke 14. He said we must count the cost. So why don't some of us respond to a call to ministry? The cost seems too high. We are not willing to give up the security we have, or at least think we have, here at home.

Jesus' final words to us were to go into all the world and preach the gospel. Yet, more than ninety percent of all Christian ministry is taking place right here in the United States. Why? Is it because this is where it is most needed? No. Not that it isn't needed here, but most of us count the cost as being too high to go to the rest of the unsaved world. So, the first hindrance we see to obeying God's call on our lives is our not wanting to give up our security.

Now look at verse 6. Here we see God speaking of anyone who has planted a vineyard. What does a vineyard represent? It is something into which we have sown. It could be our career, something for which we have been saving a long time, or anything else we have put a lot into. Perhaps we could label these as the "cares of the world." He is saying that if we have cares that are more important than the call of God, He will release us to go home and take care of them. He is not condemning us for this, but rather trying to find out just where we are in our commitment to Him.

In the seventh verse He asks, "*Has anyone become pledged to a woman and not married her?.*" Now I don't believe He is speaking here about a married couple. When you are called to ministry, you are called as a couple. God doesn't call just one to go running off, leaving a spouse at home. You are called as a couple. Rather, He is speaking to those who won't accept God's call on their lives because they don't want to leave a girl or boy friend, a grandchild, close relatives or whoever, to serve God. Our loved ones can be a hindrance to our call, not only because we may have to leave them, but because they can strongly influence our decision and commitment. Remember, Jesus said that we must hate our loved ones, in comparison to our love for Him. If we don't, they will be a hindrance to our service to Him.

Finally, in verse eight, He asks, "*Is any man afraid or fainthearted?*" Fear is a very powerful force, but what is the root cause of most fear? It's self-preservation. Some of this is good, but if it controls our lives and hinders God's call, it must be overcome. I know of those who are afraid to fly, to ride in a boat or even to drive on a high bridge. Here again, remember what Jesus said in Luke 14. We must even hate our own lives.

God wants us to be committed to Him and not back down. I would rather be in the most dangerous situation and know I am in the will of God, than to be in the most comfortable place on earth and be out of His will. God desires us to be committed to Him and His will. The communists have been more committed than most Christians. They have done more in a little over 70 years than we Christians have done in nearly 2000 years. They have won more people to their false doctrine in these relatively few years than we Christians have been able to win to the Truth since the time of Christ. And why? Because they were committed to their cause. They were willing to lay down their lives for what they believed.

We must make a "commitment check" on ourselves. What is our level of commitment? To what are we willing to be committed? Jesus wants us to become His disciples; but to become His disciples, He says we must hate other things and even our own lives and lifestyles. He also told us to be realistic about our commitment, to sit down and count the cost. Now this doesn't mean we are to throw up our hands and say, "No way. I can't do that." Rather, He wants us to be honest with ourselves, and when we see where we are lacking in our own commitment, to ask God to help us. Ask Him to help our "want to." We don't have to do it all on our own. Remember the father who came to Jesus and said, *"I do believe; help me overcome my unbelief!"* (Mark 9:24) Jesus didn't turn His back on him. No, He met him where he was. And Jesus will meet you where you are also.

A lot of people have criticized Peter because he got out of the boat and tried to walk on the water, only to look around at the circumstances and start to sink. But we know one thing about Peter; he was committed. The others didn't even get out of the boat. And Jesus didn't let him drown. He reached out His hand and helped him. That is what God is asking of us, that we commit ourselves to Him and "get out of the boat," even if it seems like a foolish thing to do. If we are open and honest, He is always there to help us where we fall short. But we must have this commitment within our own heart if we are to reach **the heart of God**.

Remember what the Lord said to the church of Laodicea. He said, "*I know your deeds, that you are neither cold nor hot. I wish you were either one or the other! So, because you are lukewarm--neither hot nor cold--I am about to spit you out of my mouth.*" (Rev 3:15-16) Why would He rather that we were cold than lukewarm? It is because when we are cold, at least we are committed to something. The church today is full of lukewarm Christians who are not committed to anything. God doesn't want any half-way commitments. He wants all or nothing. That may sound strong, but remember this -- when we give Him our all, He will give us His all. And that gives us an unlimited potential.

The Bible speaks in several places about God's wine press. Jesus is asking us if we are willing to go through His press. To be of value to Him we must sometimes be squeezed, to bring forth the "wine" that God is looking for. It takes commitment to go through the wine press and to let all of our impurities be pressed out. But when we do submit, the pure wine will flow.

God is looking for a new wine, and that only comes by our going through His press. A commitment is a decision, a decision that says, "I have decided to follow Jesus, no turning back."

Jesus said in Luke 9:62, "*No one who puts his hand to the plow and looks back is fit for service in the kingdom of God.*" He is looking for a total commitment, not one that goes along for a while and then starts looking back. This doesn't mean that He is going to kick us out of the kingdom. But during the time we are looking back, we are not fit for it. Remember the children of Israel, while they were going through the forty years in the wilderness. They kept "looking back" to Egypt and saying, "If only we were back in Egypt, we could have...." When we start questioning God as to why things are happening in our lives, it will erode our commitment.

Remember the Bible account of Joshua and how he led the people of Israel to take the city of Jericho. He had them march around the city each day, for six days. That's all they were allowed to do, just march around the city. But that was what God had told Joshua to do. Now this took commitment. Perhaps after the third or fourth day, some of them said, "I'm not going to go walk around that city any more. It's just not accomplishing anything. I'll just stay in camp today." It took real commitment to stay with it through the sixth day, but that is what God had commanded. Then, on the seventh day, after they had marched around Jericho seven times, the priests blew their trumpets and the walls fell down. God was faithful to those who were faithful to Him. He honored those who were committed.

We have all had times when we have prayed for

something and then waited and waited and nothing seemed to happen. We started wondering whether we were right in our requests. Did we make a mistake? Were we asking in error? Yet when we look back, we see the miracles God has performed in and through us. When the pressure is on, we tend to forget these things, and we are ready to give up. That's when we are in the sixth day. God is looking for those who will persevere through the sixth day. We may be going through a purging time, but He wants us to hang on, as He has something beautiful for us.

Turn now to Hebrews 12 and see what things the New Testament says will hinder us in our commitment, and what we need to do about them. The eleventh chapter of Hebrews is the so called faith chapter in which we read about all of the great men of faith. Now the twelfth chapter begins:

> *Therefore, since we are surrounded by such a great cloud of witnesses, let us throw off everything that hinders and the sin that so easily entangles, and let us run with perseverance the race marked out for us.* Hebrews 12:1

In other words, these are the men who have gone through the sixth day and into the victory of the seventh. They are seeing the fulfillment of God. These are the faithful ones of the past who have stuck it out.

Even being men of faith, I don't believe there was a one of them who didn't doubt at one time or another. But God didn't reject them and He won't reject us when we sometimes fail. Look at what this verse is telling us. It says that we are to "*throw off everything that hinders and the sin that so easily entangles,"* and that we are to *"run with perseverance the race marked out for us."*

It takes commitment to run a race. When we run a race, we don't go out wearing all sorts of extra clothes and heavy boots. We don't carry any extra weight if we are out to win. Yet look at how many times we take the heavy weight of the cares of this world into our race of commitment. We drag along the load of our own ideas, prejudices, and unforgiveness. We bring along our judging, our criticizing, and many other weights of sin and we are still trying to run the race that God has set before us. We want to be committed, yet we can't win the race because of all this extra baggage. We can't win with all of these "briers" entangling our legs. We have to be determined to be committed. We have to make a conscious decision to put these hindrances aside.

Then in Verse Two we read, *"Let us fix our eyes on Jesus, the author and perfecter of our faith, who for the joy set before him endured the cross, scorning its shame, and sat down at the right hand of the throne of God.."* Jesus had to go through Gethsemane, so what makes us think that we too will not have to go through some kind of a Gethsemane of our own. We don't like to hear this, but if we have our heart right with God, it can be a joy, knowing that we are in His will. We are going for the ultimate fulfillment of God.

Jesus willingly gave up His place in heaven, came to earth, and suffered for each of us. What do you suppose it would have been like if He, when He was in the garden of Gethsemane, had said to His Father, "No, I just can't do this. Send the angels and get Me out of here?" Can you see how important His commitment was and how important ours is also?

Without commitment, there is no way that we can say that Jesus is our King of kings and Lord of lords. We sing these things to Him in worship, but is He really our King? We in America like to vote on everything, but a kingdom is not a democracy. We don't have a vote. The King makes all of the decisions. Why haven't we progressed further than we have as Christians? Could it be that we really haven't committed ourselves to Him, that we haven't made Him our King? And we can't truly make Jesus our Lord and King without a spiritual transformation. We must have a "heart transplant." We can't do it on our own. We must let Him change our heart. But to achieve that, we must be fully committed and willing to do whatever it takes.

We may find it discouraging to see so much empty space in our churches; but God is in control, He is going to raise up His remnant. Where are the rest? They never committed themselves. They are at home licking their wounds. But God isn't through with them yet. He isn't going to reject them. They are just going to have to go through a few harder things along the way. God wants us to know Him on a real heart level, but to do so, we must come to Him committed, really committed. It takes a decision to be committed, a decision we will have to make.

In 2 Timothy 3 we see a little more about the sixth day and how close we are to the seventh day. This is speaking of end times.

> *But mark this: There will be terrible times in the last days. People will be lovers of themselves, lovers of money, boastful, proud, abusive, disobedient to their parents, ungrateful, unholy, without love, unforgiving,*

slanderous, without self-control, brutal, not lovers of the good, treacherous, rash, conceited, lovers of pleasure rather than lovers of God-- having a form of godliness but denying its power. Have nothing to do with them. 2 Timothy 3:1-5

Does that sound like what we might read in any newspaper today? Don't we see such things on the TV news? Note what the Word says in the first verse. It says, *"in the last days."* It is saying that these are the things we can expect to see in the last days before Jesus' return to earth. Do we realize how close we are? If we somehow knew that Jesus would return in two months, don't you think our commitment and our priorities would change? I'm sure they would.

Why is there such a great revival going on in China? I believe it is because of commitment. I'm sure most of us have no idea of the commitment it takes just to be a Christian in China or any other country where the gospel is forbidden or restricted. It is sad that so many have to go through such rough times and persecution before getting serious about their commitment to the will of God.

God's Word says that everything that can be shaken will be. (Hebrews 12:26-27) An earthquake doesn't only shake the surface, but it shakes well below the surface. In fact that is where it starts, down in the bedrock. There is to be a great shaking and it is going to shake right to the core of the Christian world. This shaking is to disturb our comfort zone. God doesn't want us to get too comfortable where we are, so He is shaking us up a bit. Remember, God doesn't want us to settle for what is good. He wants the best.

I get letters each week from ministries all over the country, and most of them say about the same thing. "Help me, I am about to go under." They underline and highlight at the right places to get my attention. What is this all about? It is man trying to do it on his own, man looking to man rather than to God for help. This is part of God's shaking in the last days. He is going to keep on shaking until we say, "Okay God, it's your ministry. Do with it what You wish." He knows if we need to go someplace and if He wants us there, He will supply the resources for us to get there. If it's not of God, we must learn to just let it go. If He doesn't build the house, it's built in vain. We must let it fall.

We must recognize that it is God that is doing the shaking. We often say that the devil is after us, but if we blame the devil for the shaking that God is doing, we will miss the whole point. Perhaps the primary thing within us that God is shaking is our commitment. We think we are committed but when He shakes us, only true commitment will stand. A false commitment will crumble under the shaking. What God wants of us is a commitment that will stand any shaking He may bring or allow. God is asking each of us, "Are you really committed? Are you ready and willing to do whatever I ask of you?" If our answer is anything but an unqualified YES, then we must admit it to God and let Him help us make our commitment what it should be. We can't do it on our own, but with His help, all things are possible.

The kingdom of God is like a large picture puzzle in which each of us is a piece. Through our commitment to God's plan for our lives, we will fit perfectly into the puzzle, but without it, there will be a void left where we were meant to fit. God knows where you and I are to fit into His plan, and regardless what we think about our talents or lack thereof, He knows exactly where we belong. He made us, and His place for us in the kingdom is a perfect fit for the way we are made. As we find our place and commit it to God, we will find more fulfillment and satisfaction than in anything else we could do on earth. I believe there is a "smile" in the heart of God when He hears us singing from our heart, "I have decided to follow Jesus, no turning back, no turning back. Though none go with me, still I will follow, no turning back, no turning back."

CHAPTER 5

POWER IN UNITY

But the LORD came down to see the city and the tower that the men were building. The LORD said, "If as one people speaking the same language they have begun to do this, then nothing they plan to do will be impossible for them.

Genesis 11:5-6 (emphasis added)

This opening Scripture from the book of Genesis shows God's reaction to the people who were building the Tower of Babel. He didn't like what they were doing, as they were trying to reach to heaven in their own strength. But in this small discourse, God made a very profound statement. He said that because they were "*one people*," that is they were in unity, "*nothing they plan to do will be impossible for them.*" Do we see the significance of this? Do we really understand what God is saying? **When we are in unity, there is nothing that we cannot do or accomplish!** It is for this reason that the enemy's main thrust against the Body of Christ has always been to cause division. Just look at how many denominations we have and how many believe their doctrines are the only truth, separating them from other believers over small differences of interpretation. Even within denominations, we see competition; there is no room for competition in the kingdom of God.

Noted Christian author, A.W. Tozer, wrote, "The triumph of individualism is the arch enemy of mission accomplishment." In over 20 years of full time ministry, I have come to realize the truth of this statement. The devil, the enemy of our soul, seems to realize this also. He constantly encourages us to be individualistic, out of our desire to be recognized or feel important. If this continues unchecked, we soon find ourselves caught up in, or even causing, strife and division. We then try to justify it as "our righteousness," helping God set things right.

Strife and discord, to any degree, are the opposite of unity. In the wisdom of Proverbs, God's Word makes it clear how He feels about strife. As discussed in Chapter 2, Proverbs 6:16-19 speaks of six things God hates and seven that are detestable to Him. The seventh thing mentioned was "*a man who stirs up dissension among brothers.*" Why does God detest one who stirs up dissension? Because He knows that it destroys unity.

God's heart is revealed in Psalm 133:

*How good and pleasant it is when **brothers live together in unity**! It is like precious oil poured on the head, running down on the beard, running down on Aaron's beard, down upon the collar of his robes. It is as if the dew of Hermon were falling on Mount Zion. For there the **LORD bestows his blessing**, even life forevermore.* Psalm 133:1&3 (emphasis added)

When we are in unity, we can accomplish anything, and God orders a blessing. Do you know that when God orders a blessing, we will receive a blessing? If the church could really get hold of this principle, we would see blessings poured out bountifully, more than we could ever imagine or hope for. We might even see the Great Commission accomplished in our generation.

Most of us over the years have referred to the prayer Jesus taught us in Matthew 6:9 as the Lord's Prayer. Although this seems to be a universal tradition, it is not biblical. We must examine that verse carefully. If we do, we will notice it begins, "*This, then, is how you should pray...*" If this is how we are to pray, then this is our prayer, the believer's prayer, not the Lord's prayer. Jesus gave it as a model of how we are to pray.

The true Lord's Prayer is actually recorded in the seventeenth chapter of John. The apostle John probably knew Jesus on a heart level better than anyone else. There are many things for which Jesus could have prayed, but here He prayed for those who were His. I believe that we can see much of the heart of God in this prayer. Note who and what seem important to Jesus here.

*"My prayer is not for them alone. I pray also for those who will believe in me through their message, **that all of them may be one**, Father, just as you are in me and I am in you. May they also be in us so that the world may believe that you have sent me."* John 17:20-21 (emphasis added)

Jesus is praying not only for His disciples who were with Him at that time, but *"for those who will believe in me through their message."* That's us! He was praying for us, also. And what was He praying? *"that all of them may be one."* He prayed that we, His believers, His church, would have unity. Why? So that we might be one with Him and the Father, as they are one with each other. If we are in unity, we can accomplish His work and His will here on earth, and when we do so, we will be blessed.

Continuing on in this passage, Jesus prayed:

*I have given them the glory that you gave me, **that they may be one as we are one: I in them** and you in me. **May they be brought to complete unity** to let the world know that you sent me and have loved them even as you have loved me.* John 17:22-23 (emphasis added)

Do you see what Jesus desires for us? He wants us to *"be one"*, united, just like He and His Father are one. He was in perfect unity with His Father, and He wants us to be in the same unity with Him and with each other. Jesus prayed for us to *"be brought to complete unity"*. Jesus understood the importance of unity in His people. If it was this important to Him, it should also be to us.

The Book of Acts records the birth of the early church, the Body of Christ. In the opening chapter, Jesus promises power when the Holy Spirit comes upon us, power to be witnesses -- witnesses locally, in outlying areas and to the uttermost parts of the earth (verse 8). When was this promise manifested? There had to be the fulfilling of a condition, a condition we see clearly in Chapter 2, verse 1. On the Day of Pentecost, they were all together; they were in unity. Then God released supernatural power and anointing as Peter preached, and 3000 souls were added to the Body that day. Now that's what I call revival!

Going on to verses 42 through 47 of the same chapter we see the same thread of unity, woven through this First Century Church.

> *They devoted themselves to the apostles' teaching and to the fellowship, to the breaking of bread and to prayer. Everyone was filled with awe, and many wonders and miraculous signs were done by the apostles. All the believers were together and had everything in common. Selling their possessions and goods, they gave to anyone as he had need. Every day they continued to meet together in the temple courts. They broke bread in their homes and ate together with glad and sincere hearts, praising God and enjoying the favor of all the people. And the Lord added to their number daily those who were being saved.*
> Acts 2:42-47

There was a unity and devotion to the apostles'

teaching, to their fellowship, in the breaking of bread and in prayer. *"All the believers were together* [in unity] *and had everything in common."* (v44). They *"continued to meet together,"* they *"ate together,"* and they praised God together. And what was the result? *"And the Lord added to their number daily those who were being saved."* (v47). That was the outcome, REVIVAL. As I have traveled and ministered in many nations, and especially in Russia, I have seen this proven over and over again. Where there is unity among the believers, there is revival.

In the sixth chapter of Romans, the Bible compares our baptism with Jesus' death and resurrection. It says that we are buried with Him, that is our old nature, and raised again with Him into the newness of life. Then in the fifth verse it says, *"If we have been **united with him** like this in his death, we will certainly also be united with him in his resurrection."* (emphasis added). This is true unity. We are united with Christ, through baptism, both in His death and in His resurrection. If God said that the people of Babel could accomplish anything because they were united, how much more we should be able to accomplish when we are united with each other and with Christ.

Continuing on in Chapter 12 of Romans, we discover a very clear picture of unity, as it relates to the Body of Christ.

> *Just as each of us has one body with many members, and these members do not all have the same function, so in Christ we who are many form one body, and each member belongs to all the others. We have different gifts, according to the grace given us. If a man's gift is prophesying, let him use it in*

proportion to his faith. If it is serving, let him serve; if it is teaching, let him teach; if it is encouraging, let him encourage; if it is contributing to the needs of others, let him give generously; if it is leadership, let him govern diligently; if it is showing mercy, let him do it cheerfully. Romans 12:4-8

In this revelation, we come to understand that we are all given different gifts, often referred to as "motivational gifts." These gifts are for a purpose, for as we work together in unity we complete the Body of Christ. No one is an island unto himself; no one has it all. I believe God created each of us differently, to come together as one, representing the fullness of Himself here on earth.

We are admonished to *"live in harmony with one another"* (verse 16). On one of our first mission trips into Russia, we had the privilege of seeing an opera in Moscow. It had been many years since we had heard live classical music. When we first arrived, the orchestra was tuning up and sounded awful. Each musician was "doing his own thing" and I wondered if any good music could ever come out of it. Then the conductor came forward, and with a tap of his baton, they immediately began to play in perfect harmony. That noise, when played in harmony, was the most beautiful sounding music I had ever heard.

I believe Jesus, sent by His Father, has been "tapping His baton" for some time now, waiting for the harmony of His church to become beautiful music to the heart of God.

God's desire for unity in the Body is revealed

further in the fifteenth chapter of Romans.

> *May the God who gives endurance and encouragement give you **a spirit of unity** among yourselves as you follow Christ Jesus, so that **with one heart and mouth** you may glorify the God and Father of our Lord Jesus Christ.   **Accept one another,** then, just as Christ accepted you, in order to bring praise to God.* Romans 15:5-7 (emphasis added)

We need to see three very important principles of unity. First, we see that there is a *"spirit of unity"*, into which we must come. Second, unity must again and again be born in our hearts. And third, we must accept everyone for who they are, not because of their performance.

We find in First Corinthians:

> *I appeal to you, brothers, in the name of our Lord Jesus Christ, that all of you **agree** with one another so that there may be no divisions among you and that you may **be perfectly united** in mind and thought.* 1 Corinthians 1:10 (emphasis added)

I don't see how it could be put more plainly. The Word is to be *"sharper than any two-edged sword, and piercing as far as the division of soul and spirit,"* (Hebrews 4:12 NAS). Yet today, neither we nor the world see much evidence of unity in the church. Unity must begin with agreement. Jesus said, *"Again, I tell you that if two of you on earth **agree** about anything you ask for, it will be done for you by my Father in heaven." Matthew 18:19* (emphasis added). Now that is potential power! If the church, the pastors and leaders, the missionaries, and all other Christian ministries would grasp this principle, we would see blessings and favor released from God beyond anything that we can imagine.

To further illustrate the principle of unity, First Corinthians speaks of the practice of sharing communion or the Lord's Supper. In the tenth chapter, we see:

> *Is not the cup of thanksgiving for which we give thanks a participation in the blood of Christ? And is not the bread that we break a participation in the body of Christ? Because there is one loaf, we, who are many, are one body, for we all partake of the one loaf.* 1 Corinthians 10:16-17

The Word is telling us that there is just one "*loaf*", Jesus Christ, and if we share in Him, "*we who are many, are one body.*" We are to be one, in unity, because we "*all partake of the one loaf.*" Why is there so little unity in the church today? Is it any wonder that we are not able to make any significant impression on the world when we can't even get along with one another? The Bible tells us over and over again that power comes from unity. We are to be Christ's body here on earth. As Christ is One, so are we, His body, to be one.

> *Consequently, you are no longer foreigners and aliens, but fellow citizens with God's people and members of God's household, built on the foundation of the apostles and prophets, with Christ Jesus himself as the chief cornerstone. In him the whole building is **joined together** and rises to become a holy temple in the Lord. And in him you too are*

being built together to become a dwelling in which God lives by his Spirit. Ephesians 2:19-22 (emphasis added)

It may sound too simple, but I see God's Spirit too big to be contained in just one of us. He needs us all and we need to be joined to each other. If a contractor, in building a brick wall, just stacked one brick upon another in the form of a wall, without using mortar, where would the strength be? It's hard to imagine a contractor attempting such a project. We all realize that pressure of any kind would cause the wall to crumble. This Ephesians text emphasizes that we are to be joined together. Unity is the needed mortar to build a dwelling place suitable for our living God.

In the fourth chapter of this same epistle we read:

As a prisoner for the Lord, then, I urge you to live a life worthy of the calling you have received. Be completely humble and gentle; be patient, bearing with one another in love. Make every effort to keep the unity of the Spirit through the bond of peace. There is one body and one Spirit-- just as you were called to one hope when you were called-- one Lord, one faith, one baptism; one God and Father of all, who is over all and through all and in all. Ephesians 4:1-6

What a statement of unity! God's Word encourages us to "*live a life worthy of the calling.*" Why? That we might "*keep the unity of the Spirit.*" We are to be in unity, not just with each other. We are also to be one with God the Father, one with Jesus, and one with the Holy Spirit. That's unity; but how can we ever obtain such unity? Read on in this chapter.

> *It was he who gave some to be apostles, some to be prophets, some to be evangelists, and some to be pastors and teachers, to prepare God's people for works of service, so that the body of Christ may be built up until we all reach unity in the faith and in the knowledge of the Son of God and become mature, attaining to the whole measure of the fullness of Christ.* Ephesians 4:11-13

God placed gifted people in the Body of Christ for a purpose. He gave us apostles, prophets, evangelists, pastors and teachers to build up the Body of Christ and prepare us for our intended service. We are to be built up until we *"reach unity in the faith."* Do we see how really important unity is?

Look now at the second chapter of Philippians where we find a formula for unity.

> *If you have any encouragement from being united with Christ, if any comfort from his love, if any fellowship with the Spirit, if any tenderness and compassion, then make my joy complete by being like-minded, having the same love, being one in spirit and purpose.* Philippians 2:1-2

If we are to be *"one in spirit"* with each other, we must have the same mind, the same love, and be intent on the same purpose. That is, we must be in agreement with one another, especially regarding spiritual things, and we must have the same love, the love of God. There is no room in the Body for division over doctrinal matters. It's no wonder that the non-churched people about us are not attracted to the church, when we all claim to have **the** answer, yet all have a different one.

In the letter to the church at Colossae, the Bible defines how we are to act if we *"have been chosen of God."*

> *Therefore, as God's chosen people, holy and dearly loved, clothe yourselves with compassion, kindness, humility, gentleness and patience. Bear with each other and forgive whatever grievances you may have against one another. Forgive as the Lord forgave you. And over all these virtues put on love, which binds them all together in **perfect unity**.* Colossians 3:12-14 (emphasis added)

Note what he says in the fourteenth verse. In addition to all these things, we are to put on love, because it will bond us in unity. There is nothing that brings us into unity like love. Even with this cursory look at the scriptures, it is obvious that the Body of Christ must have unity if we are to accomplish God's plan for our lives here on earth. Without it, we are doomed to failure. With unity, there is nothing that we cannot accomplish.

All through God's Word, we have seen how crucial unity is to the Body of Christ. I must say, however, that even unity requires balance. It is unity in God's will that is the key, not unity in man's ideas. God draws the line when we begin to compromise His Word or the basic doctrines of the faith. Where we may need to compromise is in our personal ideas about His Word. We must see that our individualism can be the enemy of the accomplishment of God's mission. God says that real unity comes when we, with the right heart motivation, unite to accomplish His will on earth. That is His heart's desire. Yes, only through unity can we come close to reaching the true heart of God.

CHAPTER 6

GENUINE RELATIONSHIPS

If we claim to have fellowship with him yet walk in the darkness, we lie and do not live by the truth. But if we walk in the light, as he is in the light, we have fellowship with one another, and the blood of Jesus, his Son, purifies us from all sin.

1 John 1:6-7

There are many types of relationships, all of which revolve around personal need. We are all created so as to need genuine relationships for our lives to be complete.   The kingdom of God is built around relationships.   Romans 14:17 says that the kingdom of God is **righteousness, peace** and **joy** in the Holy Spirit. These each speak of relationships: righteousness, the right relationship with God; peace, the right relationship with one another; and joy, the right relationship with our inner self.   That is the backbone of the kingdom of God.   When we are walking in the kingdom of God and let Him rule and reign in all areas of our lives, we will flow into genuine relationships.   Genuine relationships are a precious commodity that not everyone desires to obtain.   They are, however, what we were created for.

Jesus demonstrated genuine relationships with His disciples and with all those to whom He ministered. His whole life was built on relationships, not on laws or rules or religion.   **Christianity is not a religion; it is a relationship**, a genuine relationship with the Lord Jesus Christ and with other believers.   Most of today's problems within the Body of Christ are the result of weak or wrong relationships.

The closer our relationships, however, the harder we may be tested.   God often puts us together so that we will rub the sharp corners off each other.   That is the way we grow.   If we are in the will of God, we will desire close relationships.   It may not be easy; many times it will be hard.   But when we have close, genuine relationships with one another, we will find that our relationship with God will take on a much deeper dimension.

Relationships revolve around personal needs. Needs that are met build relationships; unmet needs erode relationships.   This is true in the whole Body of Christ, in an individual church or fellowship, and in the family. The principles are the same.

God designed us to have several kinds or styles of relationships. Let's look at four of them here.

STYLES OF RELATIONSHIPS. First there is the COOPERATIVE STYLE of relationship. This relationship begins with a mutual commitment to meet each other's needs. It must be developed. It is the reason that Jesus is training us, building us up, and discipling us, to meet other people's needs. It doesn't always have to be on the spiritual level; it can also be very practical. We need to develop more emphasis on reaching out and touching others and serving them. Serving is one of the motivational gifts mentioned in the twelfth chapter of Romans, and is likely the greatest of them all, though we seldom hear it taught in the church.

Some of us may wonder if we really fit anywhere in God's family or ministry. We ask, "Is there a place for me?" We may have tried this or that and failed. Nothing we have done has amounted to anything. First of all, you must understand that God has not programmed any of us for failure. What we look on as failure may well be just a mid-course correction.

Imagine, if you will, a large jig-saw puzzle on a card table and you are a child who can just barely see over the edge of the table. You see yourself as one of the pieces, and you know that you will fit somewhere in that puzzle, but you don't know where. The puzzle isn't complete enough for you to make out the picture or the image on your piece. You try to fit your piece in anywhere there is a hole, and being cardboard, your piece gets a little dog-eared.

Now this is how we are in the Body of Christ. We try to fit ourselves into the puzzle before the right time and we get a little dog-eared. Because we can't see well from our vantage point, we have a very distorted picture of what we are looking at. But when we reach the point that we will say, "Okay, Father God, You fit me in," then He, who looks down from heaven and has a perfect view of the whole puzzle, will know exactly where we fit. At the right time and in the right place, He picks up that dog-eared piece, smooths it over, and places it into the puzzle. He then looks down at the picture and says, "Now that's a beautiful and complete picture."

Each one of us has a place in God's "puzzle." We may have been going through all kinds of things. Sometimes we take our frustrations out on our brothers and sisters because we don't understand, but God has designed us to be a part of His overall picture. When we are in the right place at the right time, we will fit. We each have individual gifts and characteristics, some with sharp edges, but God can and will refine us until we fit perfectly.

This we see as the cooperative style of relationship. We have joint developments and solutions to problems. We become productive; we get more done. There is a personal commitment, and we continue to strengthen our relationships. This is the type of relationship that God has designed and desires us to have.

Unfortunately, most of us find ourselves in a different style of relationship -- the second kind, which we will call the RETALIATORY STYLE. I sometimes refer to this as an SOS relationship. When a ship is in trouble, it sends out an SOS or distress call. When we are in a retaliatory style of relationship, we also radiate an SOS. In this case, however, the SOS stands for Selfishness Overrides Servanthood.

Let's look at some of the characteristics of a retaliatory style of relationship. First, we attempt to make others conform to what we want. We demand that others meet our needs. When they don't, we become aggressive in our actions toward them. Other people become objects in our way. We want to get something done. We say to ourselves, "If you will go along with what I am doing, then I will have a relationship with you, but don't get in my way." We don't see people with their own needs. We know that this is not the relationship that God wants for us, but it is the relationship in which most of the people of the world are walking. That is why so many marriages are breaking up and so many families are dysfunctional.

These relationships become a struggle for domination. We justify our need to dominate the other person by telling ourselves that we are smarter or better than he is, so we should lead or dominate him. We do this at work, in our family relationships and even in our church family. This then leads to a continual conflict. In the end, there will be a winner and a loser in a retaliatory style relationship.

When it reaches this point, it develops into the third type, the DOMINATION STYLE of relationship. The loser gets controlled by the winner, and his personality becomes suffocated. There is a mutual loss of respect on both sides. We may feel that when we are dominating another, they have respect for us. We may even think they respect us out of fear, but the loss of respect is mutual, and without respect, there will be no genuine relationship. The loser's creativity and skills wither and dry up. He then resorts to manipulation, which only adds to the problem. He finds that he must manipulate to get what he wants. This is never God's way. There is real danger in manipulation. God's Word relates the controlling of another's will with witchcraft. The loser concludes that the situation is hopeless and there is no way out. He then stops trying to get his needs met, and there is no relationship at all.

This leads to the fourth and final type, the ISOLATION STYLE of relationship. We have probably all met people who have isolated themselves until they don't want to be with anyone or do anything. These people are in the need of inner healing and restoration, in order to function in any normal situation. This can be done, but if not attended to, it will lead to spiritual burn-out. They may completely lose their walk with the Lord, even their will to live.

ELEMENTS OF RELATIONSHIPS. Now that we have looked at the four styles of relationships, we will turn to the elements of a relationship. The first element consists of a set of characteristics I will call FUNDAMENTAL KEYS. The first of these keys is **commitment** to one another. Without commitment, there can be no relationship. The next is that we must have **sensitivity** to one another. Sensitivity is essential if we are to have compassion. The third key is to be willing to **submit** to one another. We must be willing to submit even when we don't completely agree with the person to whom we are submitting. We must realize that the relationship is usually more important than the task we are attempting to accomplish. A worthwhile end never justifies ungodly means. GOD IS MORE INTERESTED IN OUR RELATIONSHIPS AND

REACTIONS, THAN HE IS IN WHAT WE ACCOMPLISH.

The fourth fundamental key is the willingness to **trust** one another, and the fifth is that we need to recognize our **need** for one another. No man is an island unto himself. That is not the way that God designed us. No amount of Bible study or personal quiet time will yield all that we need. We need to be knitted together, because together we can bring forth all that God has for us and all that He intends for us to do. Finally, the sixth key is **respect**; we must have a mutual respect for one another if we are going to have a meaningful relationship.

Remember, we are looking at the elements that make up a relationship, the first element being the fundamental keys. The second element is the LOVE element. We tend to water down the word "love" in our culture. We speak of loving our car or loving our house. We love the nice weather or we love playing golf. We don't realize what a strong force love really is. It is a commitment. It doesn't just happen. Love does not control, it does not manipulate, and it does not extract for selfish gain. Furthermore, when love becomes lust, the relationship is destroyed. Love and lust are not the same thing, no matter what the world tries to tell us. This does not refer only to sexual lust. We may lust for power, control, money or many other things; but all lust kills relationships.

The next element of a relationship is COMMUNICATION. In a true relationship, we share everything openly and honestly and do not hold secrets from one another. We don't just tell a person what he wants to hear. I have found when ministering overseas, and especially in third-world countries, the people are genuinely grateful for our being there, and will tell us anything they think we want to hear. They will often try to paint a rosy picture of the growth in their church, for example, because they think that is what we want to hear from them. We have to emphasize to them the need for honesty in their communications with us. If things aren't going well, they must be open with us so that we can all work together to correct them. If we are not honest in our communications, secrets will spoil the development of our relationship.

There are two types of communications with which we must be concerned -- verbal and non-verbal. What we say verbally can take on very different meanings according to the non-verbal communication we transmit along with it. For example, if you are talking to a person about something and all the time you are with him you are looking at your watch or around the room, regardless of what you are actually saying verbally, non-verbally you are telling him that you aren't the least interested in the conversation. The way in which we communicate can make or break any relationship, so we must be very careful both of what we say with our words and what our actions say for us. We must be on guard, especially those of us in any type of public ministry, because it is so easy to get caught up in unintentional negative communication.

The fourth element of relationships is ENCOURAGEMENT. For a look at this element, turn to the first book of Thessalonians, Chapter 5.

> *Therefore encourage one another and build each other up, just as in fact you are doing. Now we ask you, brothers, to respect those who work hard among you, who are over you*

in the Lord and who admonish you. Hold them in the highest regard in love because of their work. Live in peace with each other. And we urge you, brothers, warn those who are idle, encourage the timid, help the weak, be patient with everyone. 1 Thessalonians 5:11-14

This sounds like a real, down-to-earth formula for relationships. We are to build each other up, we are to appreciate, esteem and love one another, especially those over us in the Lord, we are to live in peace with one another, we are to correct the unruly and encourage the weak, and we are to be patient with everyone.

How are we to build up and encourage each other? Look at what the Bible says in the first letter to the Corinthian church. In the fifteenth chapter we read:

Therefore, my dear brothers, stand firm. Let nothing move you. Always give yourselves fully to the work of the Lord, because you know that your labor in the Lord is not in vain. 1 Corinthians 15:58

Now that's a word of encouragement. Why? Because it promises that our work will not be in vain. This is not only an encouragement to us, but also an encouragement that we can use to help others, especially as we are building relationships. In Second Chronicles 35:2 we find another encouragement. It says, *"He appointed the priests to their duties and encouraged them in the service of the Lord's temple."* In context, this was when Josiah was celebrating the Passover in Jerusalem, and it says that he *"encouraged them* [the priests] *in the service of the Lord's temple."* There is a principle here. We are always to encourage, not tear down, those in ministry that the Lord has put with or over us. Whenever we are asking people to do things for us, we are to encourage them, even when they make mistakes.

As well as the people being an encouragement to their leaders, the leaders are also to encourage the people. In the book of Ezra we read of King Darius sending the workers back to Jerusalem to complete the rebuilding of the temple, which was started under King Cyrus. Then, after the temple was finished and dedicated, we read:

> *For seven days they celebrated with joy the Feast of Unleavened Bread, because the LORD had filled them with joy by changing the attitude of the king of Assyria, so that he assisted them in the work on the house of God, the God of Israel.* Ezra 6:22 (emphasis added)

Do you see it? True leadership assists the people. People are more important than the task. Without our understanding of this principle, we will never be able to build meaningful relationships.

The next element of relationships is INTIMACY. Actually, there are four types of intimacy which we will discuss. There is **emotional** intimacy, **intellectual** intimacy, **physical** intimacy, and **spiritual** intimacy. Emotional intimacy is to share our deepest thoughts and feelings with one another. We are often too proud to let someone else know what is going on inside of us. Why do so many ministers and church workers burn out? It is because they are too proud to go to a brother and say,

"I need your help." They have never built an emotional intimacy with anyone.

There is also an intellectual intimacy, but a relationship should never be built on this type alone. This goes for marriage partners, ministry partners, friendships, or any other relationships. Intellect by itself, is a false foundation, and relationships built upon it will be shaken and eventually fall apart.

Physical intimacy involves a gentle touch and concern. Physical intimacy may be sexual, but only in marriage. We must be very careful that our physical intimacy outside of marriage is never taken in the wrong way. But a physical touch, such as a hand on the shoulder, communicates a lot in relationships. It communicates love, caring, and a genuine concern for the other person.

Finally, spiritual intimacy involves accepting another's innermost beliefs. Even though they may seem different from your own, you must not reject the person because you don't share his or her beliefs. No matter what we may believe today, a year or two from now our beliefs will likely have changed in one way or another. We are continually growing and changing. We get so hung up on our own beliefs that we often miss real opportunities to share the love of God with another person who may believe a little differently than we do.

Some time ago, we were on a train in Russia and a young Russian girl was sharing our compartment with us. She immediately started sharing about astrology with us, all excited about being in the "third dimension," whatever that was. Now this was pretty hard for me to take, but I simply let her get it all out without saying much of anything. I didn't believe in anything she was saying, but I respected it as her belief. You must understand, most Russian people have had no religion, no Christian teaching whatsoever. It was obvious that this poor girl was searching, reaching out for something real to grasp.

When she had finished talking about her third dimension, I decided that I would tell her about the First Dimension, the Lord Jesus. This was hard for her to believe. She couldn't accept it at first. But finally she started coming to our meetings and got gloriously saved. Now if I had immediately put down her beliefs, our relationship would have been broken and this dear soul would still be living in the darkness of astrology. As it turned out, my Russian interpreter had to go back early, so this girl, just two weeks old in the Lord, went along with us and became our interpreter for the rest of the trip. She had some problems interpreting when I read from the Word, but we got her an English/Russian Bible, and with God's help, all worked out just fine.

Now we have said that a true relationship must be real, open and honest. There must be a covenant. We must make an effort to understand the other's viewpoint, and to understand who they are and from where they are coming. We must try to understand why they think the way they do. This is not what the enemy wants us to do. He wants us to judge, rather than to accept them. Relationships don't just happen. We need to put effort into them.

We are told to edify one another. Edification is the opposite of putting down. There is something in our old nature that makes us think by putting another person down, it will make us look better. That is a lie out of the pit of hell, but many people believe it. Businessmen are taught to compete, but there is no place for competition in the Body of Christ. We must understand that. We are all working for the same goal. The competitive spirit has destroyed many churches and ministries. In the fourteenth chapter of Romans we read:

> *So then let us pursue the things which make*
> *for peace and the building up of one another.*
> Romans 14:19 NAS

"The building up of one another" is just the opposite of tearing down or competing. We are to build each other up, edify each other. And we are to make a covenant not to provoke one another, not to stir up one another. We will never get something done through provoking. Our natural tendency is to push, but Jesus always leads, He never pushes.

We must also be aware that relationships are going to cost us something. A genuine relationship will cost us three things -- the first being our pride, which we need to get rid of anyway. In most cases, we must humble ourselves to make a relationship work. A relationship will also cost us our selfishness. To make a relationship work, we must value others more than we value ourselves. Third, a genuine relationship is going to cost us whatever it takes for us to change, because we will seldom build a genuine relationship without changing. This is all a part of the design of God, yet we all struggle with it.

HINDRANCES TO RELATIONSHIPS. Now there are some common hindrances to relationships. Why don't we easily make real relationships? There are a lot of synthetic relationships in the church today, but not many real ones. There are four main hindrances, and the enemy will use any or all of them to keep us from building genuine relationships.

The first of these hindrances to relationships is the **fear of being hurt** or hurt again. We may have had a bad experience, someone has let us down, and we are not going to let it happen again. But we must be realistic. We must see that this is a hindrance to relationships, and the devil will use it to destroy any relationship we might ever make. We must see this for what it is, put it before God, get it healed, and go on to build a genuine relationship.

The next hindrance is our **fear of taking risks**. Every relationship will have an element of risk, and that brings fear. If we try to build a relationship, we don't know how the other person is going to respond. We don't know if he will help or hurt us. We fear the unknown, so we're not going to take the risk of getting too close. This kind of fear never comes from God. This is anxious fear, and the Bible tells us *"Do not be anxious about anything."* Philippians 4:6. Perhaps this little acrostic will put fear into its proper perspective.

Fear is: False
Evidence
Appearing
Real

That's what fear is. It's the opposite of faith. We are so afraid of being hurt, we avoid taking risks instead of building relationships.

The third hindrance to genuine relationships is

that we **fear someone might see our inner self**. We may have hidden sins, hidden thoughts or whatever, about which we want no one else to know. We therefore avoid any close relationships where someone else may find us out. Most often, there is some hidden sin that we have not dealt with ourselves. Hidden sin not only hinders our relationship with God and with other people, it even hinders our relationship with ourselves. It must be dealt with.

Finally, the fourth hindrance to relationships is **the uncertainty of anything we cannot control**. Some of us like to have everything under control, all neat and in order. Relationships can place us in a position where we feel that we have lost control. Others are not always in order or under control themselves, so a relationship with them presents the threat of our being the controlled one. We therefore hold back and won't build the relationship, because that person is different than we are. This is where prejudice comes from.

VIOLATION OF RELATIONSHIPS. Once we have built genuine relationships, there are ways that we can violate and destroy them. To be violated is a serious thing, which most of us don't understand very well. On one of our trips to the Philippines, my wife found that her purse had been slit open and some of her things removed. She took this real hard and said it caused her to fear, which I couldn't understand at the time. She said that she felt violated. Now this was a word that I had heard many times but I didn't fully understand. When we think of someone being violated, we usually think of rape or some other violent act, but this incident with her purse was something that really ate into my wife. It wasn't until I had been personally attacked by some gypsies in Moscow that I had a better understanding of how she felt.

There doesn't need to be any act of violence for a violation to take place. There are at least four ways in which we can violate a relationship, each of which destroys a piece that can't easily be restored. First, we **criticize or run down others**. No relationship can endure for long when there is criticism or judgment. The Bible contains many warnings against judging others.

Second, we **consider ourselves either better or worse than the person or group** to which we are relating. This can go either way. We can look at them as being superior to us, or we can see them as inferior. In either case, no genuine relationship can exist. We have again violated the relationship by making a judgment.

Third, we **try to manipulate, intimidate or control**. No relationship can endure when there is a controlling spirit. And fourth, we **provoke to jealousy**, which includes being in little cliques. We notice this a lot in churches, and sometimes it is so subtle that we don't even recognize it as being a problem. This is not God's way, and we must be careful not to slip into it.

RESTORATION. There are ways to restore damaged relationships in the Body. First of all we need to recognize burnout and the need for inner healing. Christians, and especially those in any kind of ministry, are often susceptible to burnout. They are usually giving of themselves, while not taking anything back in. These especially need genuine relationships with others who can feed back into their lives and spirits.

To restore relationships, we must have compassion. Jesus always showed compassion. He gave us an example to live by in John 13:34-35 where He said, *"A new command I give you: Love one another. As I have loved you, so you must love one another. By this **all** men will know that you are my disciples, if you love one another."* (emphasis added). He is saying here that **all** the world will recognize that we are Christians if we have love, a genuine relationship, for one another.

In the first book of Peter we read:

The end of all things is near. Therefore be clear minded and self-controlled so that you can pray. Above all, love each other deeply, because love covers over a multitude of sins. Offer hospitality to one another without grumbling. Each one should use whatever gift he has received to serve others, faithfully administering God's grace in its various forms.
1 Peter 4:7-10

Look closely at the seventh verse. It says that we are to be clear minded and self controlled so that we can pray. Why? Because *"The end of all things is near."* We are in end times. Then the next verse goes on to say that **above all**, we are to be fervent in our love of one another. That is, we are to have genuine relationships. And look at the result of this principle. It will cover a multitude of sins. Sin is running wild in the world today; it is being poured out from the hand of Satan himself. We are told here that the way we will overcome sin is through fervent love, genuine relationships. Love will cover a multitude of sins.

This passage goes on to encourage us in offering hospitality and serving others. These are the things that will develop as we restore relationships in the Body of

Christ. This is what we need in the church. Romans 12:10 tells us to, "*Be devoted to one another in brotherly love.*"

THE RESULTS. Let's look at the greatest revival that ever happened. We must remember that God's plan all along has been to have a giant family, and to have genuine relationships within that family. In the preceding chapter on unity, we saw from the second chapter of Acts, how real power came into the church. It was through the relationships of the believers, and it resulted in extraordinary growth in the church, revival. When we see genuine relationships, real unity and sharing, we have the true formula for a power-filled and growing church. Relationships built on love, agape love, are relationships of the highest form.

Although the principles in these chapters on unity and relationships are key to the Body of Christ reaching God's heart, I believe they also apply to our family relationships. If we practice these principles in our marriages and families, we will bring "double pleasure" to the heart of God.

CHAPTER 7

HUMILITY, THE OPPOSITE OF PRIDE

Now Moses was a very humble man, more humble than anyone else on the face of the earth.

Numbers 12:3

Humility is the direct opposite of pride. God said of Moses that he was the most humble man on the earth. What greater honor could God have given him.? Throughout the entire Bible, both Old and New Testaments, we see God's hate of pride and His love of humility. Yet, as important as this is to God, it is where almost every one of us falls short.

As discussed earlier, the sixth chapter of Proverbs lists the six things that God hates, and the first listed is "*Haughty eyes*" (v17), which is another name for pride. Then in the sixteenth chapter, this is restated even stronger.

> *The LORD detests all the proud of heart. Be sure of this: They will not go unpunished.*

> *Pride goes before destruction, a haughty spirit before a fall.* Proverbs 16:5 & 18

To have a proud heart is an abomination to God. He hates it, and He will not put up with it. Pride will lead us to our own destruction. How many ministries have we seen fall in recent years? And what was the main cause? I believe almost every case can be traced to pride of heart. Even the sexual sins into which many have fallen, can often be traced to pride. There have likely been more ministries and individuals destroyed by pride than all other sins put together. Pride seems to be an even greater danger to those in the Christian music ministry. If that is your leading, examine yourself and take heed.

It was the sin of pride that led Lucifer (Satan) to rebel against God so many millennia ago, resulting in the sin-filled, pride-dominated world in which we live today. Let's examine the Biblical account of Lucifer's fall.

> *How art thou fallen from heaven, O Lucifer, son of the morning! how art thou cut down to the ground, which didst weaken the nations! For thou hast said in thine heart, **I will ascend***

*into heaven, **I will exalt** my throne above the stars of God: **I will sit** also upon the mount of the congregation, in the sides of the north: **I will ascend** above the heights of the clouds; **I will be** like the most High.* Isaiah 14:12-14 KJV (emphasis added)

Do you see the pride that was in Lucifer's heart? Five times he says, "I will." He wanted to do everything by his own power. He wanted to ascend into heaven and be like the most High. He wanted to be God. Now that is pride carried to the extreme. But aren't we all a little like that when we try to do things our own way, without even consulting God?

It is interesting to note that not only was Lucifer's sin the sin of pride, but it was pride that he used to tempt Adam and Eve in the Garden of Eden. In the third chapter of Genesis we read of the serpent (Lucifer) coming to Eve and telling her that she should eat of the tree, which was forbidden by God. Note how he tempts her as he says:

*"For God knows that when you eat of it your eyes will be opened, and **you will be like God**, knowing good and evil." When the woman saw that the fruit of the tree was good for food and pleasing to the eye, and also desirable **for gaining wisdom**, she took some and ate it. She also gave some to her husband, who was with her, and he ate it.* Genesis 3:5-6 (emphasis added)

The devil didn't tempt Eve by telling her how good the fruit of the tree would taste. He didn't even tell her how healthy it would make her. Instead he appealed to her pride and said, "*you will be like God.*" And what was Eve's reaction to this suggestion? She saw that the fruit looked good and that it was "*for gaining wisdom.*" Why would Eve want to be like God or to be wise? PRIDE!

Nothing seems to have changed much from the time of this original sin until now. We still want to have something, do something, or be someone outside of Christ. We are still tempted by the same sin as Adam and Eve.

Even after being in slavery for many years in Egypt, the people of Israel were quick to lose their humility and become proud. In the eighth chapter of Deuteronomy, Moses reminds the people how God had humbled them in the wilderness and let them be hungry (v3). Then he said:

> *Be careful that you do not forget the LORD your God, failing to observe his commands, his laws and his decrees that I am giving you this day. Otherwise, when you eat and are satisfied, when you build fine houses and settle down, and when your herds and flocks grow large and your silver and gold increase and all you have is multiplied,* **then your heart will become proud** *and you will forget the LORD your God, who brought you out of Egypt, out of the land of slavery.* Deuteronomy 8:11-14 (emphasis added)

How often do we become humble and cry out to the Lord when we are hungry and in need, but as soon as He has helped us, we again become proud? During the period of the kings, a young man of sixteen, Uzziah, was made king in place of his father, Amaziah. Uzziah ruled in Jerusalem for fifty two years. *"He did what was right in the eyes of the LORD, just as his father Amaziah had done."* (2 Chronicles 26:4). But look at how pride ended up destroying him.

> *But after Uzziah became powerful, his pride led to his downfall. He was unfaithful to the LORD his God, and entered the temple of the LORD to burn incense on the altar of incense.* 2 Chronicles 26:16

Here was a king that had everything going for him, but he let pride get in the way of his continued success. He went into the temple to burn incense, which only the priests were allowed to do. Then, when the priests confronted him, he became enraged with them. As a result of Uzziah's pride and rebellion, he was struck with leprosy, which he had until his death. God simply will not tolerate pride!

The second chapter of Isaiah speaks of the idolatry of the house of Jacob. Then in the eleventh verse we read:

> *The eyes of the arrogant man will be humbled and the pride of men brought low; the LORD alone will be exalted in that day. The LORD Almighty has a day in store for all the proud and lofty, for all that is exalted (and they will be humbled),*
>
> *The arrogance of man will be brought low and the pride of men humbled; the LORD alone will be exalted in that day,* Isaiah 2:11-12 & 17

In these verses we see God humbling the man who is proud and arrogant. If we are not humble on our own, God will humble us. I don't know about you, but I would rather be humble on my own and receive the praises of God than to be proud and have Him humble and abase me.

In the time of Hosea the prophet, the people of Israel had turned to the worship of idols, of molten silver images. God rebuked them through Hosea, and then note what He said about their pride:

> *When I fed them, they were satisfied; when they were satisfied, they became proud; then **they forgot me***. Hosea 13:6 (emphasis added)

What was the result of their pride? It made them forget the Lord. Can we see how pride will lead to all kinds of sin? When we become proud, we want to trust in our own wisdom and strength. But when we cut God out of the loop, we will soon forget Him altogether.

Jesus had much to say about pride while He walked with His disciples and taught the multitudes. For example, in the seventh chapter of Mark, He has just explained to His disciples the parable illustrating that it is what comes out of a man's heart that defiles him rather than what he eats. Then starting with verse 21 we read:

> *"For from within, out of the heart of men, proceed the evil thoughts, fornications, thefts, murders, adulteries, deeds of coveting and wickedness, as well as deceit, sensuality, envy, slander, **pride** and foolishness. All these evil*

things proceed from within and defile the man." Mark 7:21-23 NAS (emphasis added)

Note the things Jesus lists as defiling man. He mentions evil thoughts, fornications, thefts, murders, adulteries, coveting, wickedness, deceit, sensuality, envy, slander and foolishness. This is a pretty complete list of what we normally think of as the sins of man. But look at what else he listed right along with them. PRIDE! He places pride right there in the same list as fornications, murder, adultery and all the rest, and it was on the top of the list of the six things that God hates. Do we see how God looks at pride? He hates it.

Not all pride is wrong. As we see in Jeremiah, it is pride in self that the Lord hates.

This is what the LORD says: "Let not the wise man boast of his wisdom or the strong man boast of his strength or the rich man boast of his riches, but let him who boasts boast about this: that he understands and knows me, that I am the LORD, who exercises kindness, justice and righteousness on earth, for in these I delight," declares the LORD. Jeremiah 9:23-24

As we can see, it is alright to boast if our boasting is in the Lord, not in ourselves.

In his letter to the Galatian church, Paul says, *"But may it never be that I should boast, except in the cross of our Lord Jesus Christ, through which the world has been crucified to me, and I to the world."* Galatians 6:14. Paul understood the evil of self-pride and the value of pride in the Lord.

As much as God hates pride, He loves the humble. God placed humility as a prerequisite for the Jewish people to bring burnt offerings to Him. In Leviticus we see the requirements God placed on those who bring offerings on the Day of Atonement, the most holy day of the Jewish calendar.

> *"On exactly the tenth day of this seventh month is the day of atonement; it shall be a holy convocation for you, and **you shall humble your souls** and present an offering by fire to the LORD.*

> *"If there is any person who will not humble himself on this same day, he shall be cut off from his people."* Leviticus 23:27 & 29 NAS (emphasis added)

The Day of Atonement was also known as the "day of national humiliation" because it was the day in which all the sins of the people and the nation were brought before God. But note that God insisted that each person humble himself **before** he brought his offering and received forgiveness. The one who would not humble himself would be cut off from his people.

We all know the story of the people of Israel wandering in the wilderness for forty years. We know that this was the result of their refusing to enter the Promised Land when God told them to. Look at what else He tells them through Moses as to why He kept them in the wilderness so long.

> *Remember how the LORD your God led you all the way in the desert these forty years, **to humble you** and to test you in order to know*

*what was in your heart, whether or not you
would keep his commands.* Deuteronomy
8:2 (emphasis added)

He says it was "*to humble you.*" In other words,
the people of Israel had to become humble before they
would get another chance to enter into the Promised
Land. He then elaborates further on this in the
sixteenth verse where he says, "*He gave you manna to eat
in the desert, something your fathers had never known, to
humble and to test you....*" God didn't even allow them
to feed themselves. It must have been humbling for
them to have to depend on God for everything, but that
is what He desires for all of us.

There is a passage in Second Chronicles that we
hear quoted often today by those who are praying for
our nation. It reads:

*If my people, who are called by my name, will
humble themselves and pray and seek my face
and turn from their wicked ways, then will I
hear from heaven and will forgive their sin
and will heal their land.* 2 Chronicles 7:14

Note that the first requirement God puts on His
people is to humble themselves. If we expect God to
heal our land, and I don't think any of us will disagree
that it needs healing, we must first humble ourselves.
God isn't going to hear our prayers as long as we are
proud and arrogant. He is looking for a humble people
who will turn from their wicked ways and pray. That is
the only way He will hear and answer us from heaven.

Both the Psalms and the Proverbs have a lot to
say about the rewards of humility. The following is just

a sample, but it will illustrate how God feels about the humble and how He will reward them.

> *O LORD, Thou hast heard the desire of the humble; thou wilt strengthen their heart, Thou wilt incline Thine ear.* Psalm 10:17 NAS

> *He guides the humble in what is right and teaches them his way.* Psalm 25:9

> *But the humble will inherit the land, and will delight themselves in abundant prosperity.* Psalm 37:11 NAS

> *When pride comes, then comes disgrace, but with humility comes wisdom.* Proverbs 11:2

> *Better to be lowly in spirit and among the oppressed than to share plunder with the proud.* Proverbs 16:19

> *Humility and the fear of the LORD bring wealth and honor and life.* Proverbs 22:4

> *A man's pride brings him low, but a man of lowly spirit gains honor.* Proverbs 29:23

Jesus had a lot to say about humility. If we are His disciples (His disciplined followers) we can learn much from Him. Jesus said to His disciples, "*Take my yoke upon you and learn from me, for I am gentle and humble in heart, and you will find rest for your souls.*" Matthew 11:29. Jesus has always been our perfect example of humility.

In the section of the Sermon on the Mount often

referred to as the Beatitudes, Jesus alludes to humility as He says, "*Blessed are the poor in spirit, for theirs is the kingdom of heaven.*" (Matthew 5:3) Here we see the poor in spirit as teachable, sensitive, not self-sufficient, but humble. Again in Verse 5 He says, "*Blessed are the meek, for they will inherit the earth.*" It is important to understand that meek doesn't mean weak. Quite to the contrary, it is strength under control, with humility towards all men.

When the disciples came and asked Jesus, "*Who is the greatest in the kingdom of heaven?*" (Matthew 18:1), He did a very unusual thing. He called a child forward and said, "*I tell you the truth, unless you change and become like little children, you will never enter the kingdom of heaven. Therefore, whoever humbles himself like this child is the greatest in the kingdom of heaven.*" (Verses 3 & 4)

In the 20th chapter of Matthew, Jesus shows us that the greatest is the one who serves others. He says, "*whoever wants to become great among you must be your servant,*" (Verse 26). Again in Matthew 23 He says, "*The greatest among you will be your servant. For whoever exalts himself will be humbled, and whoever humbles himself will be exalted.*" (Matthew 23:11-12)

In sharing the parable of the Pharisee and the tax collector, as recorded in Luke 18:9-14, Jesus makes clear the danger in thinking that we are humble just because we are religious or spiritual leaders. We must be willing to look deep into our own hearts and examine ourselves to determine what is true humility.

The apostle Paul also gives us an example of how one can grow in humility. Early in his ministry we see Paul saying, "*But I do not think I am in the least inferior to* those 'super- apostles.'" 2 Corinthians 11:5. In his other letter to the Corinthian church he said, "*For I am the least of the apostles and do not even deserve to be called an apostle, because I persecuted the church of God.*" 1 Corinthians 15:9. There was quite a difference in attitude between these two letters. But let's continue on with Paul as he matured through the years of his ministry.

A few years later, in his letter to the Ephesians, Paul wrote, "*Although **I am less than the least of all God's people**, this grace was given me: to preach to the Gentiles the unsearchable riches of Christ,*" Ephesians 3:8 (emphasis added). Note the change here. He now doesn't even want to consider himself equal even to the other saints, let alone the apostles. Then, even later in his ministry, he wrote to Timothy, "*Here is a trustworthy saying that deserves full acceptance: Christ Jesus came into the world to save sinners--of whom I am the worst.*" 1 Timothy 1:15. Do you see the progression? Paul goes from considering himself not inferior to the most eminent apostle to calling himself the foremost of all sinners. It appears that with increasing maturity, Paul obtained increasing humility. That is how it should be with all of us.

In Micah 6:8, God shows us clearly what He desires and expects of us.

> *He has showed you, O man, what is good. And what does the LORD require of you? To act justly and to love mercy and to walk humbly with your God.*

CHAPTER 8

DISCERNING THE KINGDOM OF GOD

Your kingdom come, your will be done on earth as it is in heaven.

Matthew 6:10

When Jesus' disciples asked Him to teach them to pray, He taught them a very simple yet profound prayer, part of which is recorded above. As mentioned earlier, while we usually call this the Lord's Prayer, it is really the disciple's or believer's prayer. It is for us to pray. First, He taught them to pray that the Father's name would be hallowed or made holy. This we looked at in Chapter 3.

However, look at the very next thing in this prayer --
"your kingdom come, your will be done on earth as it is in heaven." As mentioned before, Jesus spoke more about the kingdom of God than anything else in the Bible. He mentioned it more than 100 times in the gospels alone. He must have felt the kingdom of God and our understanding of it to be very important. If we are honest with ourselves, we will realize how little we know about the kingdom of which Jesus spoke so much.

What is it that Jesus was asking us to pray regarding the kingdom? He said that we were to pray for God's kingdom to come **here on earth**. Now you may say, "Wait a minute. I thought the kingdom of God was in heaven and we were to see it when we die." Well that's just part of the truth. His kingdom is in heaven, and always has been, but that is not what He is asking us to pray for. I believe God's heart desire is for His kingdom to be established here **on** earth and also to be established **in** earth (in these earthen vessels, our bodies).

What is this kingdom of God that is to be established here on earth? I am sure you have read that the kingdom of God is *"righteousness and peace and joy in the Holy Spirit"* (Rom 14:17). I strongly believe there is much more to it than that. I believe that is not really the definition, but rather the fruit, the result of the kingdom. What is a kingdom? A kingdom is not a democracy. A kingdom is an absolute rule, an autocracy. The king has absolute power to rule as he pleases, and everyone in that domain is subject to that rule. The word "kingdom" is derived from "king's dominion."

As I began to realize how may times Jesus spoke of the kingdom of God, my heart's desire was to gain a

deeper understanding of what this was that was so important to Him. We have already established that a kingdom is a form of government, a government of absolute rule. Jesus said a couple of unusual things about His kingdom. He said that it was "*not of this world*" (John 18:36). He also said, "*The kingdom of God does not come with your careful observation, nor will people say, 'Here it is,' or 'There it is,' because **the kingdom of God is within you.**"*
(Luke 17:20-21)

I believe Jesus is speaking of our innermost being, the place where our will, our desires and our "want to" originate. The Word of God refers to this as the heart of man or simply our heart. We have already discussed how God is looking for a heart-to-heart relationship with us. Now we see how it all ties together; **the kingdom of God is the government of God ruling the heart of man**.

This is quite a revelation. It is so simple yet so profound. It is the foundation and fulfillment of our salvation. Yes, Jesus has done it all for us on the Cross; but we need to press in to all He has done for us and become all He desires us to be. Jesus said, "*Not everyone who says to me, 'Lord, Lord,' will enter the kingdom of heaven, but only he who does the will of my Father who is in heaven.*" (Matthew 7:21). This bothered me the first few times I read it. Then I began to understand the kingdom of God and realized that God wasn't picking favorites in a sort of "heavenly lottery". If He truly rules our hearts, we can't help but want to do His will and come into His kingdom.

God is the absolute Ruler and wants us all to be subject to His rule. This is the kingdom that we were told to pray for. But unlike other kingdoms, it is voluntary; God never forces His rule on anyone. God had a plan for the earth when He created it, and that plan has never changed. His plan was not just for us to go to heaven when we die. God's plan is that we have a fulfilling relationship with Him here so that His will can be done here on earth, just as it has always been done in heaven. The kingdom of God is already here. It is our privilege and responsibility to show it to others.

> *From that time on Jesus began to preach,*
> *"Repent, for the kingdom of heaven is near."*
> Matthew 4:17

One of the very first things Jesus preached was that the kingdom of heaven [God] is at hand. And He continued to preach it for His entire earthly ministry. It should be noted that Matthew chose to speak of the "kingdom of heaven," while the other gospel writers spoke of the "kingdom of God." Both mean the same thing. The Kingdom of God is a lifestyle; it is something spiritual, not physical. That is why no one can see the Kingdom unless he is born again. We don't have to die and go to heaven to find God, to talk with Him, or to fellowship with Him. He came from heaven to earth (in the form of Jesus) so that we could know Him here. We who are born again are in the kingdom of God now.

In the Book of Acts, after Jesus' death and resurrection, we read:

> *After his suffering, he showed himself to these*
> *men and gave many convincing proofs that he*
> *was alive. He appeared to them over a period*
> *of forty days and spoke about the kingdom of*
> *God.* Acts 1:3

So, the kingdom of God was not only one of the first things Jesus preached, **it was also the last**. He obviously felt it important for all His disciples, both then and now, to understand the kingdom.

It is hard for us to understand how Jesus can be both in heaven, at the right side of the Father, and here on earth, within each believer. The things that the Father wants us to know about Jesus are the things about Him (Jesus) that are like Him (the Father). We don't need to know what He **looks** like -- we need only to know what He **is** like. When we trust in Jesus, He builds into us a portion of each of the characteristics of His character and ability.

In the fourth chapter of Matthew we read, "*Jesus went throughout Galilee, teaching in their synagogues, preaching the good news of the kingdom, and healing every disease and sickness among the people.*" Matthew 4:23. Note the apparent connection between His teaching about the kingdom and the healing of the sick. He preached the kingdom and He healed "*every disease and sickness among the people.*" Wholeness and healing are a part of the kingdom of God.

Everything of the kingdom, however, will not be "*righteousness, peace and joy.*" In the book of Acts we read: "*We must go through many hardships to enter the kingdom of God,*" (Acts 14:22). There will be tribulation (pressure) on all believers who try to enter the kingdom of God. I believe that many modern-day evangelists do a great disservice to new believers by only painting a rosy picture of the Christian life. Then, the first time a trial comes, they give up and fall away. There may be righteousness, peace and joy in the kingdom of God, but there will also be trials and tribulation. We must be prepared for both.

The kingdom of God was revealed when Jesus came up from the waters of baptism and God said, *"This is my Son..."* Matthew 3:17. Jesus walked in willing obedience all of His life. When we truly find and enter into the kingdom of God, we too will want to walk in obedience, not because we have to, but like Jesus, it will be because of our love and respect for the Father. We will want to.

Jesus used simple parables, well understood by the people of His day, to illustrate the great value of the kingdom of God.

> *"The kingdom of heaven is like treasure hidden in a field. When a man found it, he hid it again, and then in his joy went and sold all he had and bought that field. Again, the kingdom of heaven is like a merchant looking for fine pearls. When he found one of great value, he went away and sold everything he had and bought it."* Matthew 13:44-46

Jesus taught that one would give up everything he had for the kingdom of God. Then in Matthew 21:43, just after telling a parable about the wicked tenant farmers, He warns, *"Therefore I tell you that the kingdom of God will be taken away from you and given to a people who will produce its fruit."* He was talking to the Jewish people, warning them that if they didn't produce good fruit from their lives, He would take the kingdom away from them and give it to others, the Gentiles. I believe He also meant that for us today. If we don't bear good fruit, that is, spread the gospel and make disciples, He will remove the kingdom from us and we will not enter into all He has prepared for us. Could He have been referring to the apathy in much of the church today, or the lavishing of God's goodness on ourselves, rather than sharing it with those in need? Are we bearing fruit?

In the fourth chapter of Luke we read:

But he said, "I must preach the good news of the kingdom of God to the other towns also, because that is why I was sent." Luke 4:43

Here Jesus is telling us of His mission on earth. He was sent to proclaim the kingdom of God. Wherever Jesus preached, the multitudes would try to get Him to stay. They never wanted to let Him leave them. But Jesus knew that the gospel of the kingdom had to be preached everywhere. He kept moving from place to place so that all could hear. Isn't this exactly what we are called to do? We were never intended to get comfortable in our own little churches and just keep to ourselves. Jesus said that we were to, *"Go into all the world and preach the good news to all creation."* Mark 16:15.

Note what Jesus says to Nicodemus, a ruler of the Jews, in the third chapter of John:

"I tell you the truth, no one can see the kingdom of God unless he is born again. How can a man be born when he is old?" Nicodemus asked. "Surely he cannot enter a second time into his mother's womb to be born!" Jesus answered, "I tell you the truth, no one can enter the kingdom of God unless

he is born of water and the Spirit. John 3:3-5
(emphasis added)

You must be born again in order to **see** the
kingdom, but unless you are born of the Spirit, that is of
the Holy Spirit, you cannot **enter** into the kingdom of
God. When we are born of the Spirit, we come closer
to letting God have the absolute rule in our lives. You
may say,"I have asked Jesus into my heart; isn't He ruling
there?" But I ask you, honestly, "Does He have absolute
rule? Does He rule every aspect of your life? Your time?
Your thoughts? Your money?" Or do you still have a
few 'pockets of resistance'?"

I saw a good example of this when we were in
the Philippines. The Philippine Islands are a group of
about 7100 separate islands. They are ruled by a
president, who in theory has rule over all 7100 islands.
There are, however, some resistance groups who have
rebelled against the president and have assumed rule
over some of the islands. One such pocket of resistance
is the western portion of the island of Mindanao, the
Philippines' second largest island. This area is ruled by
a group of Islamic rebels, who are trying to seize
control, in rebellion against the president. They want to
make the island of Mindanao an independent Islamic
state.

How is this an example of our own lives? The
kingdom of God is to be the government of God, ruling
the whole heart of man. Each of us, however, has these
pockets of resistance that we haven't subjected to God's
rule. In many places, the scriptures tell us to press into
or seek the kingdom. It's not easy to give ourselves
completely to the kingdom of God. It takes effort. If we
are really honest with ourselves, we'd have to admit that

He doesn't rule everything in our lives. But Jesus said, *"The time has come...The kingdom of God is near."* (Mark 1:15) We need to make every effort to come into its fullness.

In the United States, we are so intent on being a democracy that we want to vote on everything. But that is not the kingdom of God. We don't have a vote in God's kingdom. God created us, knows all that we are to be, and desires to bring us into it. That's the kingdom of God, His government ruling the whole heart of man, not just part of it, but his whole heart.

If this is God's intent for us, how do we find His kingdom? Jesus tells us to *"seek first his kingdom and his righteousness, and all these things will be given to you as well"* (Matthew 6:33). There are scriptures in which the Lord says that He will give us the keys to the kingdom. Let's look at the conditions surrounding this promise. In the 16th chapter of Matthew we read of Jesus asking His disciples who the people say He is, and then who they, the disciples, say that He is. Peter answered, *"You are the Christ, the Son of the living God."* (v16) Jesus responded to Peter by saying that it was His Father in heaven who had revealed that to him. He then went on to say:

> *"And I tell you that you are Peter, and on this rock I will build my church, and the gates of Hades will not overcome it. I will give you the keys of the kingdom of heaven..."* Matthew 16:18-19 (emphasis added)

Jesus promised Peter the **keys to the kingdom**. Why? It was on his confession of who Jesus really was. It was upon Peter's confession that Jesus was the Christ, the Son of God, that Jesus offered him the keys to the kingdom. In fact, He says that it is upon this revelation and declaration of His divinity that He will build His church. Can we see that? His true church is founded on the knowledge of who Jesus is. Now what is this kingdom to which Jesus offers the keys? As we have already seen, it is the full government of God. It is the complete autocratic rule of God over the lives of all creatures. It is not a democracy. It's God's complete and sovereign rule over the whole heart of man.

When we see Jesus for who He really is and submit to His government, we will enjoy the righteousness, peace and joy which are the fruits of the kingdom. Jesus talked so much about the kingdom of God, yet the church body seems to know so little about it.

There are many scriptures in which Jesus talks about our being committed to the kingdom. Look again at Matthew 6:33. *"But seek first his kingdom and his righteousness, and all these things will be given to you as well."* It takes commitment to seek the kingdom of God. We have already mentioned the scripture that says, *"For the kingdom of God is not a matter of eating and drinking, but of righteousness, peace and joy in the Holy Spirit."* (Romans 14:17) It isn't hard to be committed in order to receive righteousness, peace and joy. It's easy to seek His kingdom if that's all there is to it. But His kingdom is much more than that. It's a lifestyle. It is a commitment in itself. It is His government in our hearts, His absolute rule. When the King says something, it's done.

We must come to the realization that there are three basic kingdoms with which we have to deal. We know about the **kingdom of this world**, that is, the world's system of doing things, and we know who rules it. We are now gaining insight into the **kingdom of God**. However, there is another kingdom that we do not want to admit or talk about. That is the **kingdom of self**. This is the kingdom I have the most problem with, as do so many others. It all boils down to this. Am I willing to let God rule my heart and life completely? Yes, I'm willing to invite Jesus into my heart for my salvation. I'll even call Him Lord of lords and King of kings, but to allow Him to rule all of me, that's hard, very hard to do.

I remember for years hearing Gerald Derstine (the founder of Christian Retreat in Bradenton, Florida) say, "Jesus is in me, but me is in me too and me is my problem." Now this may not be the best English, but it sure gets the point across. It's a continuing battle; self wants to rule. That's why Jesus talks about pressing into the kingdom, which we must choose to do many times each day.

Now if God is ruling every area of our lives, that leaves no room for pride, or gossip, or strife, or jealousy or any of the things that would hinder our reaching the place that God has for us. The Word is quite clear as to what will not be tolerated in the kingdom of God. First Corinthians 6:9-10 says, "*Do you not know that the wicked will not inherit the kingdom of God?*" Also, the fifth chapter of Galatians says:

> *The acts of the sinful nature are obvious: sexual immorality, impurity and debauchery; idolatry and witchcraft; hatred, discord, jealousy, fits of rage, selfish ambition, dissensions, factions and envy; drunkenness, orgies, and the like. I warn you, as I did*

before, that those who live like this will not inherit the kingdom of God." Galatians 5:19-21

If God has absolute rule in our lives, we won't want to do or be these things and we won't need any excuses for anything in our behavior. We are guided in all things by God. Perhaps none of us has fully obtained this, but Jesus said that the kingdom of God is here, at hand. That is why He spoke more about the kingdom of God than about anything else. It is here and it is available to every born-again believer. This is the ultimate of what God wants for us, His prized possession. **Yes, Father God, Your kingdom come!**

CHAPTER 9

THE HIGHEST FORM OF WORSHIP

Therefore, I urge you, brothers, in view of God's mercy, to offer your bodies as living sacrifices, holy and pleasing to God--this is your spiritual act of worship.

Romans 12:1

In recent years, we have experienced a beautiful new expression of worship in our services, not only here in America, but even in some of the remotest parts of the world. We have seen countless variations on what we call worship, some of which we might call extreme. It seems that some have even begun to worship worship.

I am in no way making a judgment of any of the many forms of worship. True worship should be an individual expression of love and gratitude to God from the heart. However, I'm well aware of the devil's tactics. When he can't stop a good thing, he pushes it to extremes. In Russia, we've seen services with up to two hours of singing and less than fifteen minutes for the Word. Then the pastor would ask, "Why don't the people stay in the church?" These were new believers and when the emotions (the fluff) wore off, they had no solid foundation on which to stand.

I personally welcome the beautiful new expressions of worship, but it must be kept in balance. I've been moved to tears as I've seen Christians in the Ukraine, who have no material goods, with hands held high singing, "Give thanks with a grateful heart..." This surely must be a sweet fragrance to the Lord. These new believers are maturing into a solid church, founded on the Word of God.

Many times after a great worship service, after being in the presence of God, it was hard for me to understand how we simply go home and feel and live just like we did before we came. Something seemed to be missing! Through the above scripture from Romans 12, God began to reveal a very important principle of worship. We are to offer ourselves as living sacrifices. That is true worship.

Worship is so much more than singing, praising or even dancing before the Lord. I'm beginning to see that God wants us as living sacrifices. That scripture in the King James version ends with, "*a reasonable service*." It is interesting that the different translators interpreted the word "service" and "worship" the same. This gave me insight into God's heart, that He desires that we sacrifice ourselves to service. That is our reasonable worship.

If we really love God, we should always strive for a higher form of worship. Not too long ago, a young man on our worship team named Chris, stepped forward and sang a song that he had written. It cut deep into my innermost parts. I'll never forget it as I suddenly realized that this was the key to higher worship. The song was "*Obedience is The Highest Form of Worship.*"

The pastor asked him to sing it again at the close of the service. For nearly a half hour, not one person moved or even spoke. The only sounds heard were those of quiet sobbing as we all realized that God had spoken to us. I couldn't think of anything else the rest of the day. God began to deal with me on the importance of obedience to Him. If giving ourselves as a sacrifice is reasonable worship, and His Word speaks of obedience being better than sacrifice (1 Samuel 15:22), then surely obedience must be the highest form of worship!

When the desire and willingness of our hearts is to be fully obedient to God and His Word, we achieve the highest form of worship. Then, and only then, can we touch the heart of God and tap into all the blessings He has stored up for us.

From Genesis to Revelation, God's Word tells of His desire for obedience, not out of compulsion, but from a willing heart. Many today are speaking of and looking for revival, but the only real revival will result from a return to obedience. That is what God is looking for in His family, the church.

I would now like to take you on the longest journey on earth -- the journey from the head (mind) to the heart. Most Christians in America are exposed to a lot of good teaching, but it seems to have little effect on their lives. It just resides in their heads. We must get it from the head to the heart before God can effectively use us.

It was always God's plan for us to obey. Beginning with Genesis 2, we see how disobedience first opened the door for sin. We read of the beautiful garden, and of the two options placed on the first residents of that garden. There was a tree of life and a tree of the knowledge of good and evil. God's first call for obedience was when He told His creation that they could take of the one tree but not of the other.

And the LORD God commanded the man, "You are free to eat from any tree in the garden; but you must not eat from the tree of the knowledge of good and evil, for when you eat of it you will surely die." Genesis 2:16-17

We can see God's expectation for obedience from this incident in the garden. The consequences were predictable. I don't believe that it was ever God's intention for man to know evil. Evil was there, but God wanted to protect us from it so that He could have a perfect heart-to-heart relationship with us. He knew that as soon as man knew evil, that relationship would be polluted and His original plan could not be fulfilled.

We read in Chapter Three what happened.

When the woman saw that the fruit of the tree was good for food and pleasing to the eye, and also desirable for gaining wisdom, she took some and ate it. She also gave some to her husband, who was with her, and he ate it. Then the eyes of both of them were opened [to evil], and they realized they were naked; so they sewed fig leaves together and made coverings for themselves. Genesis 3:6-7

When Adam and Eve both partook of the tree, God ordered them out of the garden. They could no longer partake of the tree of life. They had made a choice, the wrong choice. They couldn't have both. We must still learn this today. We can't play with the world and have the spiritual blessings at the same time.

God called us from the very beginning to be obedient, and He warned that blessings or cursings would follow, according to how we responded. Obedience is at the heart of God. He is not a hard task master; He wants only the best for us. As I discussed in Chapter Two, God doesn't want us to be good; He wants us to be the best.

We read about God's first call on man's life in the twelfth chapter of Genesis.

The LORD had said to Abram, "Leave your country, your people and your father's household and go to the land I will show you. I will make you into a great nation and I will bless you; I will make your name great, and you will be a blessing. I will bless those who bless you, and whoever curses you I will curse; and all peoples on earth will be blessed through you." Genesis 12:1-3

God called Abram (Abraham) to leave his home, his family ties, and all that was comfortable to him, and to go to the place that He would show him. Abraham was obedient, and God blessed him as He had promised. Abraham's faith and obedience were still spoken of thousands of years later as we read in Hebrews 11.

> *By faith Abraham, when called to go to a place he would later receive as his inheritance, obeyed and went, even though he did not know where he was going. By faith he made his home in the promised land like a stranger in a foreign country; he lived in tents, as did Isaac and Jacob, who were heirs with him of the same promise. For he was looking forward to the city with foundations, whose architect and builder is God.* Hebrews 11:8-10

Abraham obviously understood God's heart and the importance of obedience. He understood the rewards of obedience, which God continued to make available both to him and to the children of Israel long after his death. When the Jewish people obeyed God, they were blessed, when they disobeyed, they were punished. We see this principle throughout the Old Testament and it is still just as valid today. In the nineteenth chapter of Exodus we read:

> *Now if you obey me fully and keep my covenant, then out of all nations you will be my treasured possession. Although the whole earth is mine.* Exodus 19:5

Although God was speaking here through Moses to the children of Israel, He is saying the same thing to His children today. He says if we obey Him, we will be His own possession, His chosen treasure. Do we really want the favor of God? Obedience is the only way to His favor. We are to obey Him, not because we have to, not because He is going to hit us over the head if we don't, but because we love Him and want to bring Him pleasure in our heart-to-heart relationship with Him.

Look next at the twentieth chapter of Numbers. Here we find the people of Israel wandering in the wilderness of Zen and complaining to Moses and Aaron about having no water. Moses and Aaron went before the Lord, who said to them,

> *"Take the staff, and you and your brother Aaron gather the assembly together. Speak to that rock before their eyes and it will pour out its water. You will bring water out of the rock for the community so they and their livestock can drink."* Numbers 20:8

God gave Moses a clear command and expected perfect obedience. Moses assembled the people as God had commanded him, but look at what happened next.

> *Then Moses raised his arm and struck the rock twice with his staff. Water gushed out, and the community and their livestock drank.* Numbers 20:11

Did Moses obey God? What was it that God had told him to do? He said to *"speak to that rock"*. And what did Moses do? He wanted to do it the same way he had done it before. Doesn't that sound familiar? He struck it twice. "That's not so bad," you may say. Besides, God brought forth water, so Moses must have done alright. That's the way we often reason, but not God. In the next verse we read:

> *But the LORD said to Moses and Aaron, "Because you did not trust in me enough to honor me as holy in the sight of the Israelites, you will not bring this community into the land I give them."* Numbers 20:12

God honored the miracle. He said He would bring forth water and He did. There are a lot of people in leadership today through whom God is performing miracles. Seeing this, we think they must have it all together in their lives and with God, but that isn't necessarily so. God may still perform the miracles because of His Word, but He will not honor the leader who isn't obedient.

This is what happened to Moses and Aaron. Because Moses struck the rock instead of speaking to it as he was commanded, God said that they would not be allowed to enter the Promised Land. Earlier, God had told Moses to strike a rock at Horeb to bring forth water (see Exodus 17:6) and he did so, but that is not what God told him to do this time. God is not satisfied with partial obedience; He wants perfect obedience.

Because Moses did not obey God perfectly, God had to change His original plan for the people of Israel. Moses was no longer going to be the leader who would lead them into the Promised Land. Moses brought forth the water as God had commanded him, but he did it his own way, not God's way. We often miss much of what God has for us because we insist on doing things our own way. Total obedience is absolutely essential in leadership. As we discussed in Chapter Three, we must have the proper fear of God, as only such fear (reverence) will bring us to total obedience.

It is not enough to just think about obedience, giving it mental assent. It must get from our heads into our hearts before it will become a natural reaction for us to obey. In the 30th chapter of Deuteronomy we read:

> *No, the word is very near you; it is in your*
> *mouth and in your heart so you may obey it.*
> Deuteronomy 30:14

Moses is telling the people that the Word of God is never out of their reach, but rather it is right there in their mouth and heart. Why has God put His Word in both our mouth (head) and in our heart? It is "*so you may obey it.*" It isn't enough to just have the Word in our head; to be able to quote it or to sing it. The Word must be in our hearts so we can willingly obey it.

Now turn back a few chapters to Deuteronomy 26.

> *The LORD your God commands you this day*
> *to follow these decrees and laws; carefully*
> *observe them with all your heart and with all*
> *your soul.* Deuteronomy 26:16

Over and over God tells us that we are to obey Him from our hearts. The people of Israel, throughout most all of their existence, failed to see this. They had their times of great worship and praise, only to fall back into disobedience. They just didn't have it in their hearts to be obedient. Not because they didn't know the

Law, but because the Law was in their heads rather than in their hearts.

The book of Deuteronomy seems to be a gold mine of examples of obedience and disobedience. In the 28th chapter we read:

> *If you fully obey the LORD your God and carefully follow all his commands I give you today, the LORD your God will set you high above all the nations on earth.*
> Deuteronomy 28:1 (emphasis added)

Often in the scriptures, God gives us a little two-letter word that precedes His promises. He says "IF". IF you do this or that, THEN I will do what I promise. How often we grab the promises and miss the IF's; we then wonder why God doesn't answer as we think He should. But be assured, if we do our part, God will always do His.

What was God's promise to His people here? If they obey Him, He will set them above all the nations of the earth. Why do you think that America was in a position of leadership to the whole world for almost a century? It was because this nation was founded on the principles of God. And why do we see our nation slipping out of this position now? It is because we have become disobedient to those same principles.

As we read on in this chapter of Deuteronomy, we see the great blessings that God has for a people who obey Him.

> *All these blessings will come upon you and accompany you if you obey the LORD your*

God: You will be blessed in the city and blessed in the country.   The fruit of your womb will be blessed, and the crops of your land and the young of your livestock--the calves of your herds and the lambs of your flocks. Deuteronomy 28:2-4

I won't quote any further here, but all the way through the 14th verse, it tells how God will bless the people in every conceivable way, if they will only obey Him. In Verse 6 He says He will bless them when they come in and when they go out, and in Verse 8 He says He will bless their barns and whatever they put their hands to.   In Verse 11, He says they will abound in prosperity.   Do we want prosperity?   Obey the Lord. The promises are ours.   But remember, all of these promised blessings begin with IF.

While God promises unlimited blessings to those who obey Him, just the opposite is true of those who don't. Immediately following these promised blessings for the obedient, we read, starting in the 15th verse:

*However, **if you do not obey** the LORD your God and do not carefully follow all his commands and decrees I am giving you today, all these curses will come upon you and overtake you: You will be cursed in the city and cursed in the country. Your basket and your kneading trough will be cursed....You will be cursed when you come in and cursed when you go out."* Deuteronomy   28:15-19 (emphasis added)

God again uses that little two-letter word "IF". This time He says, *"If you will **not** obey"*. And like the blessings for those who obey, the curses for those who disobey go on and on, in this case all the way through the 68th verse. I don't want to dwell on the curses, because we don't have to be under them. We can obey and have the blessings instead. But never forget, there are many blessings for those who obey but even more curses for those who willfully disobey.

Leaving the book of Deuteronomy, turn with me now to First Samuel. King Saul has disobeyed God's command to totally destroy the Amalekites, in that he spared both King Agag and some of the choice livestock. As we pick up the account, he is being confronted by Samuel.

> But Samuel replied: "Does the LORD delight in burnt offerings and sacrifices as much as in obeying the voice of the LORD? **To obey is better than sacrifice, and to heed is better than the fat of rams.** For rebellion is like the sin of divination, and arrogance like the evil of idolatry. Because you have rejected the word of the LORD, he has rejected you as king." 1 Samuel 15:22-23 (emphasis added)

King Saul had disobeyed God. Note what Samuel says regarding obedience. God is much more interested in our obedience than He is in any offerings or sacrifices we might bring to Him.

Samuel then compares rebellion or disobedience with the sin of divination (witchcraft). This disobedience cost Saul his kingdom, and ultimately his life. There is always a terrible price for disobedience. Obedience, on the other hand, seems to be tied to unlimited blessings. God told King Solomon, "*And if you*

*walk in my ways and obey my statutes and commands as
David your father did, I will give you a long life."* 1 Kings
3:14. Obedience can even bring long life. Proverbs
19:16a says, *"He who obeys instructions guards his life."*

King David, a man after God's own heart, has a
reputation of being a worshiper. He knew the value of
obedience, the highest form of worship. Even Solomon
was encouraged to *"obey my statutes and commands as
David your father did,"* (1 Kings 3:14). David may have
failed a few times, but he was always quick to repent, to
seek God's forgiveness, and to return to obedience. In
Psalm 103 we read:

> *But from everlasting to everlasting the Lord's
> love is with those who fear him, and his
> righteousness with their children's children--
> with those who keep his covenant and
> remember to obey his precepts.* Psalm
> 103:17-18

Can you see what is in David's heart? He is the
one who asked God to create in him a clean heart.
David understood the blessings that came from
obedience. He wanted God to put into his heart the
righteousness and obedience He wanted. Real
obedience can only come from the heart.

It is only when we are obedient that our heart can
be completely God's. It is then that He searches us out.
When we are obedient, we don't have to search for God,
He searches for us. There is no doubt that we will fail
God now and then, but with a heart of obedience, God
can still use us. Remember Peter? He even denied
Christ on the very night He was crucified, but he was
still the one God used to preach that great sermon on

the day of Pentecost, when 3000 souls were saved. Quite a revival!

Peter and David both made mistakes, but God looked at their hearts and saw what was really there. He saw hearts that wanted to obey. We must never use this as a rationalization to disobey, but when we do slip, God is there to pick us up again. He is searching for a heart that wants to do His will. He is always looking for the right heart motivation.

Jesus not only had a lot to say about obedience, He gave us the ultimate example of being obedient. In the seventh chapter of Matthew we read a stern warning to those who are all talk but don't obey.

> "*Not everyone who says to me, 'Lord, Lord,'*
> *will enter the kingdom of heaven, but only he*
> *who does the will of my Father who is in*
> *heaven.*" Matthew 7:21

This is a hard statement. We must remember what the kingdom of God really is. As stated earlier, it is the absolute rule of God in the heart of men. When we allow God to rule every aspect of our heart, obedience will become natural to us. We have to invite Him to rule every corner of our heart, our time, our pocket-books, what we watch on TV, everything. We must have no pockets of resistance. Most of us have little corners that we won't let God rule. Our biggest problem is not the kingdom of the world, it is the kingdom of self.

Jesus didn't leave any room for partial obedience. He asked for the total. In fact, those in church leadership have an even heavier responsibility to obey and to teach others to do the same. In Matthew 5 we read:

Anyone who breaks one of the least of these commandments and teaches others to do the same will be called least in the kingdom of heaven, but whoever practices and teaches these commands will be called great in the kingdom of heaven. Matthew 5:19

Obedience doesn't come naturally to most of us. It must be practiced. We must build our lives upon it. And how do we do that? By building our lives on Jesus. He is our righteousness and only through Him can we stand. In Matthew 7 we read a parable about the foundation upon which we should build a house.

"Therefore everyone who hears these words of mine and puts them into practice [obeys them] is like a wise man who built his house on the rock. The rain came down, the streams rose, and the winds blew and beat against that house; yet it did not fall, because it had its foundation on the rock." Matthew 7:24-25

With practice, we will not fall when the storms of life come upon us. But we must have our house (life) built on the Rock (Jesus). We can only do this if we obey Him.

In Jesus' final commission to His church, recorded in Matthew 28:18-20, He gives us two key words -- GO and OBEY. He says that we are to GO, go out into all the world and make disciples. In telling us to go, He is calling for our obedience. Furthermore, in telling us to make disciples, He is telling us to teach others to OBEY. Isn't that what a disciple really is, one who is disciplined, disciplined to obey?

No one better understood the importance of obedience than Jesus. At one point when He had been teaching the people, a woman started speaking blessings upon His mother. As much as Jesus loved his mother, however, He responded, *"Blessed rather are those who hear the word of God and obey it."* Luke 11:28. Obedience to the Word of God was more important to Him than anything else in life.

Obedience seems to be a real heart-cry of God. I believe that even God has some "down time" or sad times. Remember in Genesis 6:6 how God was grieved in His heart that He had made man. He saw that man's heart was evil and that he was disobedient. This greatly grieved God. But I believe we can also give God some "up time". When we are obedient, and willingly so, I believe God feels joy over us, His creation.

As in the Old Testament, many of the New Testament promises were preceded by that little word "IF". In fact, even Jesus' promise of the Holy Spirit was preceded by IF. In John Fourteen we read:

> *"If you love me, you will obey what I command. And I will ask the Father, and he will give you another Counselor to be with you forever--*
> *Jesus replied, "If anyone loves me, he will obey my teaching. My Father will love him, and we will come to him and make our home with him.* John 14:15-16 & 23 (emphasis added)

What greater promises could we have for our obedience? Can you imagine how different our lives would be today without the Holy Spirit? But note the condition on this promise. He says, "*If you love me, you will obey what I command.*" And how can we love Him and not obey Him?

In the 23rd verse, Jesus promises more to those who are obedient than just His coming to reside in them. When I stay in a hotel for a day or more, I am residing there, but it isn't home. Jesus says here that He and the Father will make their home in those who obey. They are not to just visit us; They are to make Their HOME in us!

Reading on in the gospel of John, Jesus makes even stronger statements about those who keep His commandments (obey Him). In the fifteenth chapter we read:

> *If you obey my commands, you will remain in my love, just as I have obeyed my Father's commands and remain in his love. I have told you this so that my joy may be in you and that your joy may be complete. My command is this: Love each other as I have loved you. Greater love has no one than this, that he lay down his life for his friends. You are my friends if you do what I command. I no longer call you servants, because a servant does not know his master's business. Instead, I have called you friends, for everything that I learned from my Father I have made known to you. You did not choose me, but I chose you and appointed you to go and bear fruit--fruit that will last. Then the Father will*

give you whatever you ask in my name. John
15:10-16

Again we see that this entire discourse begins with
that same little word, "IF", but look at the promises that
follow for those who obey. They will:

- Abide in His love
- Have His joy in them
- Have their joy made complete
- Be Jesus' friend
- Know all things the Father makes
  known to Jesus
- Be chosen and appointed by Jesus
- Bear fruit that will last
- Receive whatever they ask in Jesus'
  name

In addition to all the promises related in these
verses, Jesus also equates love with laying down your life
(or lifestyle) for a friend. That takes true obedience.
Then He says, "You are My friends, **IF** you do what I
command you." There are always if's to God's promises.
We must not ignore them.

We may fool ourselves into thinking that we are
free to obey or not to obey, whichever we choose, but
that is not the case. The only real freedom comes
through obedience to God. If we ignore Him, we are
simply slaves to someone or something else. In Romans
6 the Bible tells us:

Don't you know that when you offer yourselves
to someone to obey him as slaves, you are
slaves to the one whom you obey--whether you
are slaves to sin, which leads to death, or to

obedience, which leads to righteousness? But
thanks be to God that, though you used to be
slaves to sin, you wholeheartedly obeyed the
form of teaching to which you were entrusted.
Romans 6:16-17

In other words, we can be slaves to God or slaves to sin. There are no other choices. The first results in eternal life, the other in eternal death. It's our choice.

Jesus demonstrated the ultimate of obedience when He went into the Garden of Gethsemane. He said to His Father, "You know I don't want this pain, rejection and sin. But nevertheless, I will be obedient. Father, Your will be done." Obedience isn't always easy, not even for the Son of God. There have been many men who have sacrificed their lives for a friend on the field of battle. Jesus' obedience here was much more than simply giving His life. That was the easy part. His real sacrifice on the cross was the taking of all of the world's sins upon His sinless self, so that even His Father had to turn His back and forsake Him.

That was true obedience, and it was all for our benefit. The Word reveals to us in Romans 5:19, *"For just as through the disobedience of the one man the many were made sinners, so also through the obedience of the one man the many will be made righteous."* Jesus' obedience in going to the cross brought righteousness to us all. Can't we do the same for Him and likewise be obedient?

In Philippians 2 we read:

Your attitude should be the same as that of
Christ Jesus: Who, being in very nature God,
did not consider equality with God something
to be grasped, but made himself nothing,

taking the very nature of a servant, being made in human likeness. And being found in appearance as a man, he humbled himself and became obedient to death-- even death on a cross! Philippians 2:5-8

Are we willing to be obedient to death? God doesn't ask many of us to actually be martyred for the gospel, although with some He may, but He is asking us to be **obedient to the death of self**. That's the hardest battle. If we are to be His disciples, this is what God's Word is calling us to do. Only true obedience will bring us to true holiness.

As obedient children, do not conform to the evil desires you had when you lived in ignorance. But just as he who called you is holy, so be holy in all you do; for it is written: "Be holy, because I am holy." 1 Peter 1:14-16

We started our look at obedience in Genesis, so it seems only appropriate to end it in Revelation. Turn with me, therefore, to the last chapter of the Bible.

"Blessed are those who wash their robes, that they may have the right to the tree of life and may go through the gates into the city." Revelation 22:14

In Genesis, we saw the first man and woman banished from the Garden of Eden and kept from the tree of life, because of their disobedience. Through obedience, we now have the right to the tree of life that is Jesus. But the only way we can have our robes washed white is through the blood of Jesus, made possible because of His willing sacrifice of obedience.

God desires that we worship Him in spirit and in truth, and **OBEDIENCE IS THE HIGHEST FORM OF WORSHIP.**

CHAPTER 10

TAKING JESUS' FINAL INSTRUCTIONS SERIOUSLY

Then Jesus came to them and said, "All authority in heaven and on earth has been given to me. Therefore go and make disciples of all nations, baptizing them in the name of the Father and of the Son and of the Holy Spirit, and teaching them to obey everything I have commanded you. And surely I am with you always, to the very end of the age."

Matthew 28:18-20

The crowds had gathered around Jesus on that eventful day, nearly 2,000 years ago. The anticipation was great. What words of truth would the Master share? The several weeks preceding this day had been filled with excitement for Jesus, who had been crucified and then risen from the dead. He had been seen on numerous occasions and now He was about to share His last words on earth. It was to be His final instruction to His church, our GREAT COMMISSION.

From this text, it would seem that Jesus' promise to be with us always is only valid if we GO. The Bible promises that Jesus will never leave nor forsake us, but it could be presumptuous to expect Him to help us accomplish everything we set out to do if we are not willing to fully obey Him. Jesus' last words in the Gospel of Mark were, "*Go into all the world and preach the good news to all creation...And these signs will accompany those who believe...* (Mark 16:15 & 17). What a promise -- signs following -- proof backing up faith. These are the tools Jesus left for us, authority and signs.

The question is, why has the church taken this commission so lightly? Nearly 2000 years later, much of the earth's population have not had an opportunity to hear the gospel of Jesus Christ. Are we aware of how God is working in the world today? There are many Christians and even many churches that are not aware that God is doing anything at the present time. And there are a number of places where He doesn't seem to be doing anything. There are some great moves of God underway, however, in many parts of the world. We have seen an ongoing revival in the Philippines, in Russia (the old Soviet Union) and in Red China, revival of the kind that few in America have ever seen. Look at how quickly the doors opened in the old Soviet Union, with an estimated 30 million new believers in the first three years.

Although there is a great "underground revival" going on right now in China, with circuit riders and everything, I believe that it is only the tip of the iceberg. China is a country that is about to explode with revival. These present revivals are simply a preview of a great end-times harvest. Note what the prophet Habakkuk predicted many years before the birth of Christ.

> *"Look at the nations and watch-- and be utterly amazed. For I am going to do something in your days that you would not believe, even if you were told."* Habakkuk 1:5

While Habakkuk was talking to the people of Judah, what he was predicting is just as applicable to us today. Indeed, God is doing things among the nations that are unbelievable to most Christians. These are the things promised for the last days, and we see them happening now. Note what Habakkuk said. We will not even believe it when we are told. If we are to take the Great Commission, Jesus' final instructions, seriously, we must learn to see the world as God sees it.

Perhaps a few statistics will help us see what is happening in these latter days. When I first went into full time ministry in 1976, there were about 16,400 ethnic people groups that were unreached by the gospel. During the 1980's that number dropped to around 11,000 and by the end of 1995, it was more like 2500. In 1900, only three percent of Africa was Christianized. Now, most of Africa has heard the gospel and about fifty percent are born again believers. Similar results have been achieved in Latin America and Korea. In fact, Korea is now sending out more missionaries per capita than we are in America.

Do you believe we are living in the end times? Many spend their lives arguing about the exact date Jesus will return and about this and that sign that is being fulfilled. Jesus tells us exactly when He will return. Turn with me to the 24th chapter of Matthew.

*And this gospel of the kingdom will be preached in the whole world as a testimony to all nations, and **then** the end will come.* Matthew 24:14 (emphasis added)

When will Jesus return? When the gospel has been preached to the whole world, to all nations. In the biblical sense, a nation refers to a people group. When the gospel has been preached to all people groups, all nationalities, then Jesus is coming back. There are about 150 such nations or people groups in what was the old Soviet Union alone, many of which have never heard the gospel message. When people tell me that Jesus is coming back on such and such a date, I simply say no, that's not what He said. He will not return until the Great Commission is fulfilled, until the gospel is preached to all people groups. If the church had been obedient to His instructions, I believe Jesus would have come back by now, and would be ruling the entire world. Again we see God's heart. He is willing to hold up Jesus' return to earth until all have heard the gospel message.

In John 4:34 Jesus said, *"My food is to do the will of him who sent me and to finish his work."* It is now up to us to finish this work. Can we complete Jesus' Great Commission to carry the gospel to all nations? We had better do so if we want to see His return. We can help or hinder it. Which will it be?

God has a goal for us here on earth. If His purpose was simply for us to get saved and go to heaven, we would be best off to have a machine gun behind a curtain in our churches. Then, as soon as someone gets saved, rat ta tat tat. Off to heaven. No back sliders. But He has a much bigger plan for us. It is His goal for us to reveal Him to all of His creation. That's why we are here, to bring the revelation of God, the fullness of Christ, to all people.

Look back at our opening text from Matthew 28. Jesus said that we are to make disciples of all nations. This is a command, not a suggestion. This is the great **co-mission**. That is, it is the **co-assignment** of the missionary, and of the church that stands behind him.

What is a missionary? He is one who goes out, cross-culturally, leaving his own culture and comfort zone, going to those who are completely different from himself, to spread the gospel. This is what Jesus did when He came to earth. He left His spiritual culture in heaven and came to our physical culture on earth. That was the highest missionary call.

God is looking for a womb in which to birth His plan. About two-thirds of the Bible speaks of God working through man. This is God's desire, to work through man. We go to church and other meetings to see the supernatural. We lay hands on the sick and they are healed, and we say, "Wow! Now that's supernatural, it's a miracle." It shouldn't be. It should be a natural thing if we are going in obedience to His Word. Remember, Jesus said to go into all the world and preach the gospel and that signs and wonders would follow.

We have seen a lot of what we call miracles -- the blind see, the lame walk, the sick are healed. But the greatest of miracles comes when we heed the Great Commission, and someone says, "Yes I believe, I receive Jesus into my heart." We have seen other miracles, but I don't want to dwell on them. It seems we all want to follow the miracles, but God intends for the miracles to follow us as we walk in obedience.

I have always had a great love for trains. As a young man, I wanted to live life to its fullest, and I thought that to actually drive a train would be heaven itself. I once got a chance to do so, to climb up into a steam locomotive and pull back on the throttle. We accelerated to 70 miles per hour, pulling a string of passenger cars behind us. What a thrill! It was the highlight of my life at that time.

Some years later, I joined the Navy, learned to fly an airplane, and was able to take the helm of a large sailing ship. I thought my life was really fulfilled. I had done so many of the things I had dreamed of. But after I came to the Lord and began to win souls, I found that nothing else in life could compare. It became my greatest fulfillment and satisfaction. We are often told, "You can't take it with you." In truth, there is one thing that you can take to heaven with you -- SOULS. Nothing we accumulate here on earth has any value in eternity except souls won to the Lord.

We are looking to reach the heart of God. His heart is in the Great Commission, the union of God's POWER with our GO. God could have brought whoever He wanted into the kingdom by simply using His own powers. But that wasn't His plan. He planned to use man, you and me. Do you understand that the Bible is a missionary book? Let me show you. We will start at the beginning, in Genesis the 12th chapter, and work our way to Revelation.

> *The LORD had said to Abram, "Leave your country, your people and your father's household and go to the land I will show you. "I will make you into a great nation and I will bless you; I will make your name great, and you will be a blessing. I will bless those who bless you, and whoever curses you I will curse; and all peoples on earth will be blessed through you."* Genesis 12:1-3

Now doesn't this sound like Abram (Abraham) was called to be a missionary? I believe that this is the first missionary call. Note that God gave Abram three incentives. He said, "*I will make you into a great nation and I will bless you.*" Here is the promise of blessing, because Abram was willing to go. The second incentive is in the same verse where God said, "*I will make your name great.*" Unfortunately, a lot of ministries stop at the first two incentives; they want the blessing and they want a great name.

I believe, however, that the third incentive is the one God really desires for us. He went on to say, "*I will bless those who bless you, and whoever curses you I will curse; and all peoples on earth will be blessed through you.*" This is the first place in the scriptures where we see God choosing to work through man, and He says, "I'm going to send you out and you are going to be a blessing. All of the people of the earth are going to be blessed through you."

God promised to bless all the people of the earth

through Abram. What a challenge! Abram, who later became Abraham, was to be the father of all the Jewish nations. And as the Word says, we have been grafted into Abraham's promises. The children of Israel, however, did not bless all nations. As they grew in number, they became ingrown. God had to send in kings and armies to get them out into the world. He told them not to mix, but He didn't tell them not to share.

As we look further through the Old Testament, we again find a missionary call in First Chronicles. Here we find a more general call.

> *Sing to the LORD, all the earth; proclaim his salvation day after day.* **Declare his glory among the nations,** *his marvelous deeds among all peoples. For great is the LORD and most worthy of praise; he is to be feared above all gods.* 1 Chronicles 16:23-25 (emphasis added)

Do you see the key phrase here? He says, "*Declare his glory among the nations.*" We are to tell all people of God's glory. That's our missionary calling, our Great Commission. It's interesting to see how many times the word "nations" is used in this context. People often question why we spend so much time and effort on ministering to other nations when there are so many needs right here at home. God said over and over again that we were to go to **all** the nations.

In some circles we hear a lot about fasting, but it is often looked upon simply as a way to get the Lord to do something for us. Let's look at what the prophet Isaiah had to say about a fast.

"Is not this the kind of fasting I have chosen: to loose the chains of injustice and untie the cords of the yoke, to set the oppressed free and break every yoke? Is it not to share your food with the hungry and to provide the poor wanderer with shelter-- when you see the naked, to clothe him, and not to turn away from your own flesh and blood? Then your light will break forth like the dawn, and your healing will quickly appear; then your righteousness will go before you, and the glory of the LORD will be your rear guard." Isaiah 58:6-8

God seems to be telling us that fasting is much more than just giving up something. We are to DO something. Verse seven clarifies this. *"Is it not to share your food with the hungry and to provide the poor wanderer with shelter-- when you see the naked, to clothe him, and not to turn away from your own flesh and blood?"* This is doing something for others. We are to feed them, to shelter them, and to clothe them. This can also be taken into the spiritual realm. We can feed them on the Word of God, protect them from the curses of sin and clothe them with God's love. This is all a part of the fast to which God is calling His people.

In Proverbs 28:27 we read, *"He who gives to the poor will lack nothing, but he who closes his eyes to them receives many curses."* We have a missionary friend whose motto is, "Live to Give." It is not just money we are talking about; we are talking about time, about energy, about prayer, about involvement, about life (lifestyle). Ask yourself, if you came into a lot of money, what would you do with it? Likewise, as you come into the knowledge of God's Word, what should you do with it?

Those in real poverty are the ones without a knowledge of their Lord and Savior.

On my first mission trip to Guatemala, I saw a lady stamping in the clay to make bricks. She would put straw in the mud and mix it with her feet. The local missionary told me that this lady had given her property to build the church. She now comes out every day to mix the clay and straw and put them in forms. The workers then come out to build the church from the bricks she has made. She lived in one little corner of the land. These people were so poor, and all they needed was $200 worth of tin for the roof. It made me realize how many times I had spent $200 or more on things that were of no lasting value to me or anyone else.

Like He so often does, God ends the Isaiah text we just read with a promise for those who obey. In Verse 8 of Isaiah 58, God says He will make our light shine like the dawn, our healing come speedily, our righteousness go before us, and His glory will be our rear guard. Think about it. Who is our righteousness? It's Jesus. So Jesus will go before us and God's glory will guard us from behind. Now that is a promise to get excited about!

Look now at the promises in verses nine and ten of this same chapter of Isaiah.

> *Then you will call, and the LORD will answer; you will cry for help, and he will say: Here am I. If you do away with the yoke of oppression, with the pointing finger and malicious talk, and if you spend yourselves in behalf of the hungry and satisfy the needs of*

*the oppressed, then your light will rise in the
darkness, and your night will become like the
noonday.* Isaiah 58:9-10

The Lord says that when we call, He will answer.
He is promising to answer our prayers. But notice He
puts some conditions on that promise. He says He will
answer us if we remove the yoke, the pointing finger
and the speaking of wickedness, and if we take care of
the needs of the afflicted. Again, He says we must do
something. We have to quit judging and criticizing and
gossiping about people, or we will nullify God's
promise. But if we do quit these things and take care of
the hungry and afflicted, He says that our light will rise
and our gloom will become as bright as the midday sun.
If you have ever seen the midday sun in the tropics, you
will appreciate this promise.

This text says that we are to **spend** ourselves on
the hungry. That means more than just saying a little
prayer once in a while or putting a dollar or so in the
mission's offering. We're to spend ourselves. And not
just on the physically hungry, but also on the spiritually
hungry.

Now if we do spend ourselves for the Lord, verse
eleven goes on to say, *"The LORD will guide you always."*
That too is a promise. Do you want the guidance of the
Lord? I believe we all do, but that isn't all that is said in
Verse Eleven. Let's look at the whole verse:

*The LORD will guide you always; he will
satisfy your needs in a sun-scorched land and
will strengthen your frame. You will be like a
well-watered garden, like a spring whose
waters never fail.* Isaiah 58:11

I had a problem understanding this verse at first, but I believe that this is what the Lord has shown me. Many of us have areas in our lives that are scorched. We may be suffering from burnout, from hurts or whatever, but there are these scorched areas in our lives where nothing can grow. God can minister to us in these areas. He says that He will strengthen our bones and water the dry places with a spring that will not fail.

The quickest way to recover when we are in the need of inner healing is to spend ourselves on others who are hungry or otherwise in need. It is a real call to reach out to those who want to know God. You may not find many that are hungry for God in your own neighborhood or family, but there are many who hunger for Him in the other parts of the world. Therefore, I think of these verses as a call to missions.

This Old Testament call is repeated again in the sixtieth chapter of Isaiah.

> *"Arise, shine, for your light has come, and the glory of the LORD rises upon you. See, darkness covers the earth and thick darkness is over the peoples, but the LORD rises upon you and his glory appears over you. **Nations will come to your light**, and kings to the brightness of your dawn."* Isaiah 60:1-3 (emphasis added)

If we arise and shine, the nations (plural) will come to us. But we have to arise; we have to get up and go. We must make the first move and shine forth the light of Jesus; then God will bring the nations to us, nations of hungry people, those who hunger for God.

I had the privilege of praying with a top

government official while in Russia. I didn't know his title, but I could see that he was badly crippled. Of course, all of these government officials in Russia were atheists. After I prayed for him, he said he felt so much better, that maybe God was real after all. The seed was planted. *"Nations will come to your light, and kings to the brightness of your dawn."* But not if we sit at home in our comfort zone.

In the 31st chapter of Jeremiah we read of another missionary call:

> *"Hear the word of the LORD, O nations; proclaim it in distant coastlands: 'He who scattered Israel will gather them and will watch over his flock like a shepherd.'"*
> Jeremiah 31:10

God is telling us to declare His Word in the distant coastlands. The King James translation speaks of declaring His Word in the *"isles afar off"*. It was partly this text that first convinced us to go to the Philippines, Roatan, Haiti and Jamaica -- all distant islands.

In Haggai 2:7 it says that God will shake the nations to come to Him. God is shaking the nations all over the world today. The Russians had seventy three years of shaking under Communism, but now multitudes of people from the former Soviet Union are coming to Christ. I believe we are going to see missionaries coming to the United States from eastern Europe and Russia because we are turning down what they have just discovered. The mantle is being passed from our nation to others who will receive it. We seem to be too self-centered, caught up in our own agenda, while those elsewhere, who have so little, are giving so much. Yes, there is a lot of shaking.

The whole emphasis of missionaries is changing. It used to be that a missionary went into a country and spent his life there. He would build a church and continue to pastor it for years and years. But the indigenous people would never learn to be on their own. Then, if there was a change of government, the missionaries would be thrown out and the believers would be scattered like sheep without a shepherd.

Now, we feel our call is to train the local people to be the leaders and pastors, which brings the stability that the church needs. We teach them and then they reach out to the lost. It has been said that if you give a man a fish, he has something to eat, but he will need you to provide another fish each day. If you teach a man to fish, he can feed himself for the rest of his life.

We really see the heart of the Father through Jesus as we read in the ninth chapter of the gospel of Matthew.

> *When he saw the crowds, he had compassion on them, because they were harassed and helpless, like sheep without a shepherd. Then he said to his disciples, "The harvest is plentiful but the workers are few. Ask the Lord of the harvest, therefore, to send out workers into his harvest field."* Matthew 9:36-38

Note, Jesus had compassion on them. As we mentioned earlier, the Bible tells us that Jesus had compassion on the people before He performed any miracles of healing or deliverance. This seems to be the

key to miracles, real miracles. But what is compassion?
It is more than just feeling sorry for someone. It is
putting your feet into his shoes, putting yourself in his
place. It is when we pray with compassion that God
moves. It may be hard to have compassion for everyone
in every situation, but we must develop a heart of
compassion, especially for the lost, if we are to be His
disciples.

At times we have been used of the Lord in the
ministry of restoration or inner healing. I would often
find myself crying with the people as I prayed for them.
I couldn't understand what was going on. Later I would
say, "Lord, I'm supposed to be encouraging these
people. Why am I in tears? It's not me that has the
problem." That's when the Lord started teaching me
about compassion. He was allowing me to feel the hurts
of others as He feels them. It is the heart of God that
we have compassion. It was out of this compassion that
Jesus told His disciples to *"Ask the Lord of the harvest,
therefore, to send out workers into his harvest field."*

Jesus sees the world as harassed and without a
shepherd. Even the leaders of this nation and of the
world are themselves like sheep without a shepherd.
They run from one problem area to another and don't
know what to do about any of them. There is no true
guidance anywhere in the world. That is how Jesus sees
us. If we had sent out missionaries instead of armies to
the world's trouble spots, how different the world would
be today.

We were in Durban, South Africa, in 1977. A
three-way racial conflict was going on among people
from India, the black natives, and the whites. They all
had animosity toward one another and stayed in their

own little groups. But when we went into the church, we saw people from all the different races and groups, raising their hands and praising the Lord. Riots on the street but praise in the house of God. Do we see how the gospel makes a difference? These people were praying together for unity in South Africa, and today we are seeing the fruits of those prayers.

We started this chapter with Matthew 28:18-20 where Jesus told us to GO. He said to go into all nations to preach the Gospel and make disciples. In verse twenty, He said that we were to teach them, not just get a lot of people fired up to come forward, confess their sins and then leave them. We are to teach them, disciple them. Without such teaching, many of those responding to an altar call have no idea what they have done, and will likely just slip back into their old ways after the evangelist or missionary has gone.

On our way to minister in Novosibirsk, we were told that a famous healing evangelist had been there some time before us and over five thousand people had come forward to receive the Lord. I said, "Wow, that's great!" But when we arrived, there were less than one hundred. I was told that all they did was come forward and say a prayer, mainly for healing, and then went home and went on with life as usual. In contrast, when we ministered in Volgograd, a few hundred came forward to receive the Lord after a teaching on "Knowing God." The Lord impressed upon us to stay for many days, meeting every night, teaching them the basics of Christianity, of which they had no previous knowledge. We also brought and distributed hundreds of Bibles. We knew the importance of establishing new believers in the Word.

This was in May. We left them as a small group, meeting in a room at the Cultural Center. When we came back in September, we found that same church, meeting in the Lenin Theater, filling all four balconies, and two years later, they numbered 1,200. That is what happens when people receive teaching in the things of the Lord. There is fruit, fruit that remains. That is why Jesus told us to make disciples. There are now some from that Volgograd church, who have themselves become missionaries.

In the sixteenth chapter of the gospel of Mark we read:

He said to them, "Go into all the world and preach the good news to all creation. Whoever believes and is baptized will be saved, but whoever does not believe will be condemned. And these signs will accompany those who believe: In my name they will drive out demons; they will speak in new tongues; they will pick up snakes with their hands; and when they drink deadly poison, it will not hurt them at all; they will place their hands on sick people, and they will get well."

Then the disciples went out and preached everywhere, and the Lord worked with them and confirmed his word by the signs that accompanied it. Mark 16:15-18 & 20

I have heard testimonies of missionaries who have eaten or drank something that was actually poisonous, that should have made them deathly ill, but they were not harmed in any way. Verse 20 said, "*Then the disciples went out and preached everywhere, and the Lord worked with them and confirmed his word by the signs that accompanied it.*" (emphasis added). Note that they didn't go in search of signs and wonders. They went and preached the gospel and the signs followed. When we do the work to which the Lord called us, He will cause the signs to follow.

We have proven this many times in the field. One time in the Philippines we were praying for people after the service and a blind woman came up with grey pus flowing from her eyes. I have to admit that I didn't have the faith to believe for her healing. Although I was looking at the natural, I was obedient and prayed for her anyway. A little later, as we were praying for someone else down the line, we heard a commotion and looked back to see this same woman dancing up and down and pointing to the front of the hall. She kept saying, "I can see. I can see people on the platform." All I could say was. "WOW! Do you mean, God, that You can use even me for something like that?" Praise God, He is true to His Word. We can attest to the fact that signs and wonders follow those who go into all the world and preach the gospel.

I like to look at Luke 4:18-19 as Jesus' job description. Jesus is actually quoting this from Isaiah.

> *"The Spirit of the Lord is on me, because he has anointed me to preach good news to the poor. He has sent me to proclaim freedom for the prisoners and recovery of sight for the blind, to release the oppressed, to proclaim the year of the Lord's favor."* Luke 4:18-19

As disciples of Jesus, do we not have that same job description? We are to release the captives and bring sight to the blind. The people of Russia have been blinded and held captive for 73 years; they have been told that there is no God. But to see them come out of this blindness and open their spiritual eyes has been one of my greatest joys. There isn't anything that I have seen like it in my whole life.

We again see God's heart through Jesus in Luke 10:2-3 which says, *"He told them, 'The harvest is plentiful, but the workers are few. Ask the Lord of the harvest, therefore, to send out workers into his harvest field. Go! I am sending you out like lambs among wolves.'"* It is not enough just to ask God to send out workers. He also tells us to **GO**.

There is a song I don't think many have heard and fewer sing; but I believe it is close to the heart of God.

THERE IS PEACE AND CONTENTMENT IN THE FATHER'S HOUSE TODAY.
LOTS OF FOOD ON HIS TABLE, AND NO ONE IS TURNED AWAY.

THERE IS SINGING AND LAUGHTER, AS THE HOURS PASS BY,
BUT A HUSH CALMS THE SINGING, AS THE FATHER SADLY CRIES.

MY HOUSE IS FULL, BUT MY FIELD IS EMPTY,
WHO WILL GO TO WORK FOR ME TODAY?
IT SEEMS ALL MY CHILDREN WANT TO STAY AROUND MY TABLE,
BUT NO ONE WANTS TO WORK IN MY FIELD; NO ONE WANTS TO WORK IN MY FIELD.

166

PUSH AWAY FROM THE TABLE, LOOK THROUGH
THAT WINDOW PANE.
JUST BEYOND THIS HOUSE OF PLENTY, LIES A
FIELD OF GOLDEN GRAIN.

AND IT'S WHITE UNTO HARVEST, BUT THE
REAPERS, WHERE ARE THEY?
O, IN THE HOUSE; CAN'T THE CHILDREN HEAR
THE FATHER SADLY SAY,

MY HOUSE IS FULL, BUT MY FIELD IS EMPTY,
WHO'LL GO AND WORK FOR ME TODAY?

IT SEEMS MY CHILDREN ALL WANT TO STAY
AROUND MY TABLE,
BUT NO ONE WANTS TO WORK IN MY FIELD.

Why would I say that this song represents God's heart cry? Perhaps it describes how out of balance the church of America has become. Where are our priorities? For the answer to that, look at the following statistics.

- Over 90% of Christian ministry goes on in the United States and Canada, yet we have only five or six percent of the world's population.

- In the United States, there is one Christian worker for every 230 people. In the rest of the world, there is one Christian worker for every 450,000 people.

- Ninety six cents out of every dollar given to Christian ministry is designated for use right here at home. Only four cents of each dollar goes to overseas ministry.

• More money is spent each year on Christmas wrappings than is given to all missions put together.

• More dollars are sent to the eight top TV ministries than given to all missionaries and missions organizations combined.

• Ten percent of churches in the U.S. carry out 90 percent of the mission activities.

• Eighty percent of the world's population have no Bible at all, while most of us have several.

• There are still about 2500 ethnic people groups that are considered unreached by the gospel.

While in Honduras for two years in the 1980's, I had a heart-shaking vision. I saw the face of Jesus looking down on a multitude of people. I noted that they were mostly foreigners, as I saw tears run down Jesus' cheek. The Holy Spirit said very clearly to my heart, "I am coming soon, and My people are just playing church." Is it any wonder that Jesus said, "*Why do you call me, 'Lord, Lord,' and do not do what I say?*" Luke 6:46.

As we read earlier in John 4:34, Jesus says, "*My food is to do the will of him who sent me and to finish his work.*" Do we want to see the work of God finished, so that Jesus will come back in all of His glory? In the thirty-fifth verse He goes on to say, "*Do you not say, 'Four months more and then the harvest'? I tell you, open your eyes and look at the fields! They are ripe for harvest."* This scripture was instrumental in our selling our house in order to go to Russia at a time when it was difficult to otherwise raise finances. When we got to Russia, that was exactly what we found. The fields were white for harvest. The people were hungry for anything of God. They would come up to us and ask, "Are you Americans? Can you tell us about God?" There is just nothing else like it in the world, that hunger for God.

In the first chapter of the book of Acts, Jesus promised:

> *"But you shall receive power when the Holy Spirit has come upon you; and you shall be My witnesses **both** in Jerusalem, and in all Judea and Samaria, and even to the remotest part of the earth."* Acts 1:8 NAS (emphasis added)

Jesus says that we are to be witnesses BOTH in Jerusalem and in Judea and in Samaria and in the uttermost parts of the earth. He didn't give us a choice of one or the other. We are to be witnesses in them all. This is where much of the American church has dropped the ball. Jesus was speaking from Jerusalem, but He said both in Jerusalem and in these other places, even to the remotest part of the earth. Our Jerusalem is the place we are now, our home community. Judea is the neighboring areas and Samaria represents those of other cultures. In Jesus' time, the Samaritans were considered the unlovely or undesirable people. *"The remotest part of the earth"* means just that. We are to reach all of the world for Jesus, not just the easy parts.

I have heard pastors say that they have a good missionary program; they are giving ten percent of everything that comes in to missions. I am thankful for that, but that should be only the first step. I don't believe that is what the Lord was saying here. When He said both, I think He meant that at least fifty percent is to go back out the door to reach other places of the world. I feel that this should be the goal of every church, that fifty percent of what comes in goes to fulfill Jesus' final instructions. Now this doesn't necessarily mean all to foreign missions. There are good outreaches here on the home front too, but half of everything that comes in should be used for reaching souls. I am convinced that God will bless any church that does this, and that they will never suffer financially because of it.

It took a while for the early church to reach out beyond their borders. We just read Acts 1:8; now turn in your Bible to Acts 8:1b. Here, just following the stoning of Stephen, we read, *"On that day a great persecution broke out against the church at Jerusalem, and all except the apostles were scattered throughout Judea and Samaria."* You see, we can go to our "Judea" and "Samaria" as missionaries or we can go as refugees. God can send us one way or the other. Don't say it can't happen.

When we get God's heart desire into our own hearts, Jesus will return much more to us than anything we may give up.

> *Jesus said to them, "I tell you the truth, at the renewal of all things, when the Son of Man sits on his glorious throne, you who have followed me will also sit on twelve thrones, judging the twelve tribes of Israel. And*

*everyone who has left houses or brothers or
sisters or father or mother or children or fields
for my sake will receive a hundred times as
much and will inherit eternal life."* Matthew
19:28-29

We may have felt we have had to leave a lot
behind when we entered the mission field, but God has
provided a home and family for us everywhere we have
gone to minister. We don't stay in hotels, we stay in the
homes of the people. God has never failed to care for
us when we were doing His work.

Philippians 4:19 says, *"And my God will meet all
your needs according to his glorious riches in Christ Jesus."*
We love to quote and claim this promise for ourselves.
There is a danger, however, in taking scriptures out of
context. To see what God's Word was really saying to
the church, we need to start at the fifteenth verse.

*Moreover, as you Philippians know, in the
early days of your acquaintance with the
gospel, when I set out from Macedonia, not
one church shared with me in the matter of
giving and receiving, except you only; for even
when I was in Thessalonica, **you sent me aid
again and again** when I was in need. Not
that I am looking for a gift, but I am looking
for what may be credited to your account. I
have received full payment and even more; I
am amply supplied, now that I have received
from Epaphroditus the gifts you sent. They are
a fragrant offering, an acceptable sacrifice,
pleasing to God.* Philippians 4:15-18
(emphasis added)

Paul had departed from Macedonia on a missionary trip, and was going without any support except from the church at Philippi. They were the only ones who cared about supporting missions. They continued to give support, and because of this, the great promise in verse nineteen is made. They gave, and God gave back to them. That's God's way. I am sure that this word is also for us today. If we continue to give to valid missionary efforts, God will never fail to meet our needs through Jesus Christ.

Most of us know John 3:16 by heart, but how many know 1 John 3:16? In this and the two verses following we read:

This is how we know what love is: Jesus Christ laid down his life for us. And we ought to lay down our lives for our brothers. If anyone has material possessions and sees his brother in need but has no pity on him, how can the love of God be in him? Dear children, let us not love with words or tongue but with actions and in truth. 1 John 3:16-18

Jesus laid down His life for each of us. He left the glories of heaven, took on the form of man, suffered rejection and died an agonizing death for our salvation. This we know and accept. But look what else it says. We also are to lay down our lives (or lifestyles) for our brothers. If we have material possessions and see another in need and do not help him, how can we say we have the love of God in us? Verse eighteen tells us not to love with words only, but with deed. Actions always speak louder than words.

In the 24th chapter of Luke, Jesus said:

"This is what is written: The Christ will suffer and rise from the dead on the third day, and repentance and forgiveness of sins will be preached in his name to all nations, beginning at Jerusalem." Luke 24:46-47

Here in the gospel of Luke we again find Jesus' final instructions to all who are His disciples. Although stated somewhat differently, He is still telling us to go and preach the gospel to **all nations**. This is His Great Commission (command).

After World War II, General MacArthur sent a memo to many of the Christian denominations in the United States, saying that Japan was ripe for the gospel. Very few would go, and a window of opportunity was lost. Think what it would be like today if Japan had been converted to Jesus Christ and was now exporting the gospel instead of cars, televisions and computers. The whole world might have been won for Christ. Do you see how we missed it? God intends us to think globally. We hear a lot of talk about one-world-government. And yes, we Christians want a one-world-government, but one ruled by Jesus Christ, not by man.

We see the final result of our missionary efforts in the seventh chapter of the book of Revelation.

After this I looked and there before me was a great multitude that no one could count, from every nation, tribe, people and language, standing before the throne and in front of the Lamb. They were wearing white robes and were holding palm branches in their hands.

And they cried out in a loud voice: "Salvation belongs to our God, who sits on the throne, and to the Lamb." Revelation 7:9-10 (emphasis added)

In the end, that great multitude of believers will come from **every nation**. We can either be a part of this or just sit back and watch it happen, but God's plan will be accomplished. The Word of God says so. From Genesis to Revelation we see the Bible as a missionary book. The question remains. What will we do as individuals, or together as the Body of Christ. Will we take the Great Commission seriously or will we simply take it as the "great suggestion?"

Taking the Great Commission seriously will cost us something. It may cost us our lifestyle, that "comfort zone" to which we hold so strongly, or it may cost us our material possessions. But we must remember Jesus' Words. He said, *"For where your treasure is, there your heart will be also."* Matthew 6:21

CHAPTER 11

THE OUTCOME, REVIVAL

Will you not revive us again, that your people may rejoice in you? Show us your unfailing love, O LORD, and grant us your salvation. I will listen to what God the LORD will say; he promises peace to his people, his saints-- but let them not return to folly.
Psalm 85:6-8

Here we see the heart cry of David, a man after God's own heart. We see not only the desire for revival, but for permanent revival. He says, "*but let them not return to folly.*" That is, let us not go back to the same old things, being religious, "playing church". At this point, I believe we must ask ourselves some very basic questions. What is revival and what is it not? Revival is not a series of meetings planned by man. We perhaps mock God by advertising our tent meetings or crusades with posters saying "Revival Here Tonight." Revival is not another word for evangelism. We can have evangelism without revival, but true revival will always result in evangelism. Real revival doesn't end when the evangelist leaves.

True revival must be God-initiated. It is a fresh anointing, God doing a new thing, and it is unique. Hearts are really changed, the masses are shaken, the church is renewed and many are moved to evangelism, both locally and to all the world. Many more are quickened to learn and teach the Word of God, and still others stirred to social action.

When real revival comes, we will become a unified church, a community saturated with God's presence. When real revival comes, the world will know it. Our worship will come from the heart and we will know that God desires our holiness, not just our hype.

If we look at the history of the great revivals of past centuries, jails were emptied, bars were closed and gambling halls went out of business. Why? It was not because the laws were changed or new laws passed. It was because so many people repented and gave their lives to Christ that there was just not enough business to keep them open. More important, some of these great revivals lasted for years, sending out thousands to evangelize the world. It was revival that started the modern missionary movement which is still transforming the world.

Who would have believed only a few years ago that we would be able to go into Russia and have people come up to us on the street and ask us to tell them about God? That is a miracle. And who would have believed that there would be 50 to 80 million believers in Red China? Our God is doing wonderful things right before our eyes. He is bringing revival to the hearts of many throughout the world.

The next question is **what will we do** with revival when God releases it? Will we just consume it ourselves, boasting on how big our church or ministry has grown? Will we see how many extravagant buildings we can build? Or perhaps we will just see how many meetings we can attend and how many good feelings we can receive. Oh, how revival could make us popular with our booming churches and ministries. It could be a great boost to our egos.

But **what does God desire** that we do with revival? In the preceding chapters, I have tried to express in words what God has put on my heart as being necessary for revival to come. I believe that God wants to see this great end-time harvest even more than we do. But we must be ready! God needs to know we will do what He desires with revival.

Not long ago, I had a vision about revival. In that vision, I saw churches so crowded that the pastors were calling to other churches, asking, "Do you have any room left in your church? We can't handle all that are coming in." Now that is something to get excited about! Yes, Lord, bring revival!

We must ask, are we ready for revival? Many Christians around the world are praying for revival.

Fervent prayer is essential, but we should also be asking, "Are we ready for the commitment it will require? Are we ready to care for and disciple those who are gathered? Are we ready to train and nurture the thousands of new believers that will need our help or will we simply leave them to make it on their own?" Now is the time for preparation, for the training of leaders who will fill the gap when revival comes. Once revival starts, it will be too late. The Bible speaks of the early rain and the latter rain. I believe that the latter rain refers to the coming end-time revival.

When we were in Africa in March of 1994, they were in the middle of a drought. As I approached the meeting place where I was to speak, I saw a small cloud way off in the distance. It spoke to me of the cloud "as small as a man's hand" that Elijah's servant saw when Elijah had prayed for rain (see 1 Kings 18:44). As I looked at that small cloud, the Lord impressed me that the rains of revival were on the way. I joked with a resident missionary, telling him that there was the cloud the size of my hand and it is going to rain. He said that I didn't know what I was talking about, as they were in the middle of the drought season. You can imagine what happened in the meeting that morning when the Lord brought a heavy rain while I was preaching the message, "The Rain of Revival Is On The Way." The people really got excited, especially when I told them what had happened just before the service.

As the service went on and the rains fell, I thought about how muddy it was going to be when we had to go back outside. Much to my surprise when I left the building, the rains had stopped and the ground was dry and hard as concrete, just as it had been when we went in. It had rained hard, but the rain had simply run off. The Lord showed me something from this. He said, **"The reason I am holding back revival is because My people's hearts are hardened like this ground. If I pour out the end-time rains on them now, it will just run off and go into the sea. It will not benefit anyone."** We must have hearts softened and prepared to receive revival before He will send it. God's Word says that we need to break up that fallow (hard) ground. Perhaps then we can receive revival in our hearts. Remember, revival must begin with us.

There have been great revivals in the past, and some not-so-great. Perhaps they were all potentially great. Many of these simply dissipated as quickly as they came. Why didn't they last? Because they were not focused on the harvest and on the Lord of the harvest. If a revival comes and we simply focus on ourselves, it will quickly dissipate.

The first time I went to Israel, I was fascinated by the difference in the Sea of Galilee and the Dead Sea. The waters flow from the mountains in the north of Israel and pour into the Sea of Galilee from the Jordan River. This sea is beautiful, and so clear that you can see rocks on the bottom with fish swimming around them. This same water flows back out of the Sea of Galilee, back into the Jordan, and south into the Dead Sea. It is the same water, but in the Dead Sea it is so polluted and putrid that nothing can live in it.

What is the difference? In the Sea of Galilee, the water flows in and right back out again. The Dead Sea, however, just keeps taking in but never lets anything back out. The water simply sits there and evaporates, leaving behind all its salt and other impurities. This is what is happening to much of the Body of Christ. We keep taking in and taking in but never giving anything back. If we simply focus on ourselves, rather than God's harvest, we will soon dissipate or become polluted, and not be of use for anything.

Look now at what the book of Titus says about being prepared.

> *For the grace of God has appeared, bringing salvation to all men, instructing us to deny ungodliness and worldly desires and to live sensibly, righteously and godly in the present age, looking for the blessed hope and the appearing of the glory of our great God and Savior, Christ Jesus;* Titus 2:11-13

The Bible is saying that when real revival comes, there is going to be a change on the inside. I'm talking about the fruits of revival that will show it to be real. When revival comes, we will see an even greater grace, one that will establish us in the truth of our justification through Christ Jesus. We will know that we are secure in our salvation. Ministers and church leaders worldwide, who have been lukewarm, will come under conviction and be brought to repentance, by God's grace. We will learn that God's grace doesn't mean that we can get away with whatever we want. That's not what His grace is all about. The grace that will come with revival will change us and our way of thinking.

In the twelfth chapter of Zechariah, the tenth verse, he prophesied that in the last hour, the Spirit would fall mightily on God's people, with a spirit of grace that turns them away from all worldliness. He will produce in them a cry for the purity of heart and a genuine desire for His holiness.

How are we going to recognize this revival when it comes? How can we be sure that it is real? Turn in your Bible to the seventh chapter of Matthew. Here Jesus says:

> *"You will know them by their fruits. Grapes are not gathered from thorn bushes, nor figs from thistles, are they? Even so, every good tree bears good fruit; but the bad tree bears bad fruit. A good tree cannot produce bad fruit, nor can a bad tree produce good fruit. Every tree that does not bear good fruit is cut down and thrown into the fire. So then, you will know them by their fruits."* Matthew 7:16-20 (emphasis added)

Note that Jesus says the same thing in both the sixteenth and twentieth verses; *"You will know them by their fruits."* Whenever Jesus says something twice, we had better pay attention. He was emphasizing it for a reason. He also said that the tree that bears bad fruit would be thrown into the fire. If we don't see God working in our church or fellowship, take heed. Ask yourself, "Has He cut us down and thrown us into the fire? Has God left because there was no good fruit?" He may be taking us through some trials and testing, but He won't leave us there if we really want to come out. He is a loving God, full of grace. But there must be good fruit.

Jesus had quite a few things to say about fruit. In the fifteenth chapter of John He says:

> *"You did not choose Me, but I chose you, and appointed you, that you should go and bear fruit, and that your fruit should remain, that*

*whatever you ask of the Father in My name,
He may give to you."* John 15:16

Do we understand what Jesus is saying? He says
that He has chosen us. And for what? To bear fruit,
fruit that will remain. Jesus is not looking for temporary
experiences, about which we get excited and want to
build a tabernacle. That is what Peter, James and John
wanted to do when they were on the Mount of
Transfiguration. They wanted to build tabernacles for
Jesus, Moses and Elijah. And this is what we so often
want to do. We have a great experience, perhaps we fall
out under the power of the Spirit, and then we want to
build a tabernacle on that experience and call it revival.
We want to fall out everywhere we go. It is wonderful
to feel God's power in our midst, but real revival will get
us off the floor, out the door, and into the world. Jesus
wants to see lasting fruit, fruit that will remain after the
goose-bumps have gone. I have been in many meetings
where there were great moves of the Spirit, where
people were all excited about what was happening, but
they would lose it all by the time they got home. Real
fruit will remain. It will affect our lives and everything
we do.

Turn to Proverbs 11:30. Here we read, *"The fruit
of the righteous is a tree of life, and he who is wise wins
souls."* God connects the fruit of righteousness with life.
One of our fruits, when we live righteously, will be life,
true life. Then He goes on to relate this fruit with the
winning of souls. Souls are the harvest; souls saved are
the greatest gift we can bring to God. They are the fruit
that will remain forever, for eternity.

Look now at what the book of Romans says
regarding how we are to bear fruit for God.

Therefore, my brethren, you also were made to die to the Law through the body of Christ, that you might be joined to another, to Him who was raised from the dead, that we might bear fruit for God. Romans 7:4

How are we to bear fruit for God? The Bible says that we have to die, die to the Law through Christ. We must die to ourselves, to the old self, to the old ideas and traditions. Only then can we be truly joined to Christ Jesus, raised with Him from the dead to bear true and lasting fruit. The law and traditions of man can nullify the Word of God. We may look at that church down the street and think of them as being stuck in old dead traditions, but if we are honest with ourselves, we will have to admit that we too are tied up in traditions in one way or another.

Do we realize what one of the greatest hindrances to revival is? It is simply being satisfied where we are. Being satisfied in the traditions to which we have become accustomed. We don't see revival because we are satisfied with things just the way they are. In fact, we usually fight change. Yes, **the greatest enemy of revival is our satisfaction with the status quo.**

Turn now to the first chapter of God's Word to the church at Colossae.

*For this reason also, since the day we heard of it, we have not ceased to pray for you and to ask that you may be filled with the knowledge of His will in all spiritual wisdom and understanding, so that you may walk in a manner worthy of the Lord, to please Him in all respects, **bearing fruit** in every good work*

and increasing in the knowledge of God;
Colossians 1:9-10 (emphasis added)

Paul was praying for the Colossian believers that they might please God. If we really love our wife or husband, boyfriend or girlfriend, we want to do whatever we can to please them. That is only natural. If we really love the Lord, we will of course want to please Him also. In fact, we should want to please God much more than anyone else in the world. We are so grateful for all He has done and is going to do for us, that we want to please Him in every way we can. We don't have to, we want to. So what can we do to please Him? This is what God's Word says is pleasing to Him, that we bear fruit in every good work.

In the second chapter of James we read:

You see that faith was working with his works, and as a result of the works, faith was perfected; and the Scripture was fulfilled which says, "And Abraham believed God, and it was reckoned to him as righteousness," and he was called the friend of God. You see that a man is justified by works, and not by faith alone. James 2:22-24

Now if you will allow me, I would like to substitute the word "fruit" for "works" in Verse 24. If we are doing the work of God, there is going to be fruit, and it is this fruit, along with our faith, by which we are justified. If there is no good fruit, it is not the work of God, no matter how spiritual it may look. Then, Verse 26 goes on to say, "*For just as the body without the spirit is dead, so also faith without works* [fruit] *is dead.*" You will know them by their fruits.

In my early Christian walk, after my wife was miraculously healed from a heart attack, I was so hungry for the truth of God that I was reading everything I could lay my hands on, some good and some not. I started to get confused at the conflicting teachings and asked the Lord for help. And what did He show me? "You will know them by their fruits." God seemed to imprint that word indelibly in my head. Is there good or bad fruit resulting from this ministry or teaching? Is it building up God or is it building up man? Who is being glorified? If God is being built up and glorified, there will be good fruit.

In the next chapter of the book of James we see an expansion of this same line of thought.

But the wisdom from above is first pure, then peaceable, gentle, reasonable, full of mercy and good fruits, unwavering, without hypocrisy. And the seed whose fruit is righteousness is sown in peace by those who make peace. James 3:17-18

James is talking about wisdom, wisdom from above, and he says that this Godly wisdom will produce good fruit. I often hear people say "God told me this," or "God told me that," but nothing happens. Where is the fruit? If it is God's wisdom we are receiving, there will be fruit.

Some time ago while I was ministering in Honduras, the Lord gave me a message regarding the taking of His name in vain. Everyone got real comfortable when I announced my subject, expecting another lesson on the third commandment, *"You shall not take the name of the LORD your God in vain, for the*

LORD will not leave him unpunished who takes His name in vain. Exodus 20:7. Most of us feel that this commandment simply means not to use the Lord's name as a cuss word. But when we say, "God told me this," or "God told me that," and He didn't, aren't we taking His name in vain? Do we realize how serious this is? Then, when God doesn't come through with what we claimed, we blame Him for something He didn't say in the first place. We must be careful what we say or what we claim the Lord said to us. We are to come boldly to His throne, but we must do so with fear and respect of who He is.

What kind of fruit are we to bear? There are two basic kinds referred to in the Scripture. There is a **personal fruit**, and there is **fruit from the harvest** for the kingdom of God. Regarding our personal fruit, we see it well defined in Galatians 5:22-23 which speaks of *love, joy, peace, patience, kindness, goodness, faithfulness, gentleness,* and *self-control.* These are the personal fruits that should be found in every true believer. But now I would like to focus on the fruits from the harvest for the kingdom of God.

What is the kingdom of God? As we said in Chapter 8, it is **the absolute rule of God in the hearts of men**. It is only when God reigns and rules in our lives that we can come fully into His kingdom. As stated earlier, all of the other religions of the world try to find God through head knowledge, but God wants to rule our hearts, not our heads.

In the gospel of Luke we read:

And He called the twelve together, and gave them power and authority over all the

demons, and to heal diseases. And He sent
them out to proclaim the kingdom of God,
and to perform healing. Luke 9:1-2

I want to point out a principle here. In the first verse, we see Jesus giving power to His apostles. But is power alone of any real value? If I had a car with 500 horsepower under the hood, but I just left it sitting in the garage, all that power would be of no value. I have to get it out of the garage and onto the highway before the power can accomplish anything. Now look again at verse two. Jesus didn't just give them power, He sent them out to use it. He sent them out to preach the kingdom of God and to heal the sick. This was a two-part command. It was to preach and to heal. It isn't enough just to hold great healing crusades. That is only half of the commission.

Many in the church today are running after signs and wonders. Every time there is a healing meeting, it is packed. But Jesus said that we will know them by their fruits, not by the signs and wonders. Jesus didn't send them out just to heal, He sent them out to preach the kingdom, to make new disciples.

Referring back to the 500 horsepower car, if it had a lot of carbon in the cylinders and dirt in the carburetor, it wouldn't perform very well even if we did get it out onto the highway. But what about ourselves? Do we have a bunch of junk entangling us and taking away our power? What about all the things of the world that have a hold on us, and all the junk we take in each day from TV and newspapers? Jesus gives us the power to go out and preach the kingdom of God, but we must do so as clean vessels. This is when we will see signs and wonders following. This is when we will see real revival.

When we go to Russia, we find the people so hungry for God that they will come to hear us just because they think that everyone from America must know about God. The people come and they get saved. We don't hold any huge crusades. We simply teach of the kingdom of God and the principles presented in this book, yet 30 to 40 people each night get saved. That's what revival is all about. The reason that I am excited about this end-time revival is because I've had a taste of it. During the first summer we ministered in Russia, the Ukraine and the Crimea, we personally saw over one thousand not only receive Jesus, but get well grounded in His Word.

We were staying at a hotel in the Crimea on the Black Sea, in the south part of the old Soviet Union. While we were eating in the dining room, some staff members came up to us and said, "You are from America. You must know about God. If we bring the staff together, will you tell us about God?" We said, "Sure, that's why we are here." Eight out of fourteen of them raised their hands and received Jesus right there in the hotel.

This is the hunger for God that feeds revival. People even came up to us on the train and ask if we would tell them about God and pray for them. Jesus said to go out and preach the kingdom of God and to heal the sick. We can have a great healing meeting, but without the preaching of the gospel, there will be no revival. There will be no fruit that remains. Lasting revival can only come when the desire for revival comes from the heart. God created us for a heart-to-heart relationship with Him and He is searching the earth for those whose heart desires to fulfill that relationship. *"For the eyes of the LORD range throughout the earth to strengthen those whose hearts are fully committed to him."* (2 Chronicles 16:9a).

We have looked at nine ways to reach the heart of God. I am convinced that when we truly reach His heart, we will have the key to revival. They are:

- THE RIGHT HEART MOTIVATION. Are we really serving God because of who He is, or because of what we might get from Him?

- UNDERSTANDING THE FEAR OF GOD. Do we have a reverence and understanding of who God is, and the proper respect for Him and His holiness?

- COMMITMENT. To whom and what are we committed? Are we fully committed?

- UNITY. Are we in unity or in competition with other believers and ministries?

- GENUINE RELATIONSHIPS. Are we properly related to the Body? It is only genuine relationships that will knit the Body of Christ together.

- HUMILITY. Are we walking in pride or humility?

- DISCERNING GOD'S KINGDOM. God wants to establish His kingdom here on earth, just as it is in heaven. Do we understand His kingdom?

- THE HIGHEST FORM OF WORSHIP. There is no higher form of worship than our obedience to

God.

- TAKING JESUS' FINAL INSTRUCTION SERIOUSLY. Are we going forth, revealing God to all His creation? Are we making disciples? This is not just a fruit of revival, it is what will bring a lasting revival.

Revival is on the way and God is preparing those who will be a part of it. The whole mission of the church will change as true revival comes. It will not only become a teaching station for training those who will then go out to preach the Word and bring in others, but a place that transforms lives into the likeness of our Lord Jesus. We have a big God who desires a big family. Ever since the first man chose to disobey, God has had a plan to get His family back, a family in the likeness of His only begotten Son, Jesus Christ.

So here is the "bottom line." **When we reach the full potential for which God created us, we reach THE HEART OF GOD.**